Gender

The Inclusive Church Resource

DARTON·LONGMAN + TODD

First published in Great Britain in 2015 by
Darton, Longman and Todd Ltd
1 Spencer Court
140 – 142 Wandsworth High Street
London SW18 4JJ

ISBN 978-0-232-53069-8

The article 'The Rise and Fall of Default Man' by
Grayson Perry first appeared in the *New Statesman*, 8
October 2014. It is reprinted here with permission of the
New Statesman.

A catalogue record for this book is available from the
British Library

Phototypeset by Judy Linard
Printed and bound by Imak Ofset, Turkey

Contents

Acknowledgements

Inclusive Church is grateful to all who have made this book possible.

We are especially grateful to the *New Statesman* and Grayson Perry for permission to reprint *'The Rise and Fall of Default Man'*.

In particular we would like to acknowledge the enthusiasm and support for this book from David Moloney at Darton, Longman and Todd. We would also like to express our thanks to Allison Ward for her work in compiling the indexes for the Inclusive Church Resource Book series.

We are grateful to the Churches Equality Practitioner Group for ideas and suggestions for this book series.

The Inclusive Church Resource Book series has only been made possible through the generosity of those who have contributed time, stories, reflections and resources for these books. Thank you to each contributor.

It is our hope that all that is shared here will encourage others to go further in the work of creating a more inclusive and welcoming church.

About Inclusive Church

Inclusive Church was formed in 2003. From the start, churches and individuals have signed up to the statement of belief as a way of indicating their desire to see a more accepting and open church.

The Inclusive Church
'Statement of Belief'

We believe in inclusive church – church which does not discriminate, on any level, on grounds of economic power, gender, mental health, physical ability, race or sexuality. We believe in church which welcomes and serves all people in the name of Jesus Christ; which is scripturally faithful; which seeks to proclaim the Gospel afresh for each generation; and which, in the power of the Holy Spirit, allows all people to grasp how wide and long and high and deep is the love of Jesus Christ.

www.inclusive-church.org

Introduction

*Dianna Gwilliams is currently Dean of
Guildford. Dianna was born in Colorado,
USA and grew up in California. She read
physics and chemistry at university and came
to the UK to work as a sound engineer for just
six months. Thirty five years later she is still
here. Following twelve years as an engineer
she was ordained in Southwark Diocese
where she served her curacy and then as
incumbent for 14 years. She is Chair
of Inclusive Church.*

'Mum', asked my seven-year-old brother, 'what's
sex?' My mother launched into, what seemed
to the nine-year-old me, the most far-fetched
answer possible. Some of the words she used
I understood, but many I did not, and most of
what she said made no sense to me or to my
brother. At the end of my mother's answer to
my brother's question, he replied, 'How am
I going to fit all that into this little box?' He
held up the application form for a school trip
which he was trying to complete. The section

he had reached was the one titled 'Sex' and with two boxes, one marked B and the other marked G. All he wanted to know was which box to tick. As well as teaching me to find out why questions were being asked, this story now reminds me of a time when life appeared more simple. People were either B or G, boys or girls. What we know now, almost fifty years on, is that questions about B and G refer to gender, and that B and G are not the only options. Issues of gender and sex are complex and richly textured. This complexity has as a common theme the normative power dynamic of the B or G boxes on my brother's form. This dynamic is reinforced by the faith narratives of the Hebrew Scriptures and by the peoples of the first century CE (AD) as they explored what it meant to be human, to follow the example of Jesus of Nazareth and to glorify God in all.

The language available to our ancestors is different to the language available to us. We have the language of anthropology, biology, literature, cultural studies and two thousand years of human reason and church tradition. In this book, Rosemary Lain-Priestley presents a theological reflection about gender informed by academic traditions and her own life experience. Those who have contributed their personal stories have done so in the courageous hope that there might be resonance with and encouragement for those who read them. I hope you find both.

I am a child of the American 1970s. I grew up in a family where there was an expectation that my brothers and I could find our own way of flourishing with no gender or educational bias. Two of us went to university, the other became the youngest ever licensed Master mechanic in our state, having worked hard to compress apprenticeship into only four years. My youngest brother and I followed my father into engineering. It was not until I came to the UK in 1978 that I experienced any gender bias. I was completely unprepared for it and just thought it was rudeness. However, in listening to British young women I found that it was far deeper than simple rudeness, and came to understand it as part of the consequences of the 'B or G' paradigm. This paradigm contains more than simply a binary approach to nomenclature and definition. It contains also an assumption of male as superior or complete and female as inferior and incomplete. This complex concept has led to the failure, where it occurs, to understand that when women ask for equal treatment and consideration, they aren't asking to be treated as, or considered as men, but as women, equal to men. Equally complete, equally made in the image and likeness of God, equally called to the service of others in the name of Christ.

What I hope from this book is that the resonance with the experience of many will inspire continued study and action, encourage those for whom the engagement is difficult or lonely and challenge those who might say, as I did all those years ago, 'What's all the fuss?'. What I also hope is that those who may read the book in fifty years' time will be able to look back and see how far we have come, as a society and as the church of God.

As this book is being prepared for the printers the appointment of the first woman bishop in the Church of England has just been announced. This is very good news for all the church. I hope those of you reading this book in 2065 will find the phrase 'woman bishop' as archaic as I would find 'man bishop'. That would demonstrate a good distance along the journey towards a realisation of the declaration of St Paul, that in Christ there is no division between B and G but that all are one in Christ Jesus.

PART 1
Experience

Stories from lived experience are central to this book. It would be easy to skip this section and read the theological reflection or look at the resources. The stories here are real and give voice to how the issue of gender is experienced by different people.

We are grateful to these story–tellers for their honesty. Our theological reflection and practical outworking should follow from these accounts of lived experience, so please take time to read these stories carefully.

Rachel's story

Rachel Mann is an Anglican priest, poet and broadcaster. The author of two books, her memoir of growing up trans, 'Dazzling Darkness' *was a Church Times bestseller. She is minor canon and resident poet at Manchester Cathedral and is a regular contributor to Radio 2's* Pause For Thought.

Coming Out

Before the wild splash of sex smashed into
    egg
broke the yolk of self again and again
multiplied in the red silt of amniotic sac,
back before the beginning of the breaking
of the waters, and the soft plop of head

slipping out between my mother's legs,
I was always this: the queen of high-kicks,
tottering in Manolo Blahniks, sashaying
in a thousand-watt neon billboard dress
before I could crawl.

Gender

This is what I am: the joke whispered
behind the schoolgirl's hand,
the giggled glance, the woman's stare
as she moves seats with her son,
the constant pat of slap on my chin.

Checking mirror, window, screen
for the shadow of that other one
I am and am not, the sir, er,
madam, as the crowd parts
when I click onto the tram.

Save your She-male, He-She,
keep your Tranny for bantz in the loos
pissed and new tattooed, yeah I'd do 'it',
nah, I'd puke, while I tip-tap home,
frightened you're tracking my code,

the tick of my heart,
the dress shaking my bones.
Running away from your smile
with the punch nestled inside, racing back
behind the door where mardi gras,

the swirl of frock, where high-kicks rule,
searching back, seeking the hindwaters,
before the thrusting leap of life
entered in, back before the self broke,
before I was ever this.

My childhood and adolescence were very similar to most young people growing up in a basically stable and loving UK home in the 1970s. It had the usual mixture of fear, love, triumph and failure. But I had a secret. A secret that grew within me like a painful tumour. I felt I should not be a boy, but a girl. I'd known this in a barely articulated way since I was about four. By the time I hit puberty it had become a raging internal pain. My body was changing day by day – becoming hairier, leaner, my voice and face changing. I felt like I was becoming monstrous. And I was unable to articulate this to anyone. I was sure that if I spoke to family or friends I'd be labelled 'mental' or ridiculed or bullied. The only 'person' I tried to speak to was God. Each night I'd pray. A ridiculous prayer. A small, naïve, child's prayer. A prayer which asked that somehow, overnight, God would turn me into a girl. As I entered my teens I understood how stupid this prayer was and I stopped praying. As far as I could see, either there was no God or – more likely – he was a sadist who enjoyed the unhappiness of people.

One doesn't need to be an academic to understand that the concept of 'gender' is complex. All of us grow up negotiating the societal, cultural and religious expectations connected with notions of 'boy', 'girl', 'man' and 'woman'. The meanings of those words is encoded and decoded in countless ways, from dress, speech, deportment and so on. Yet, growing up trans makes one particularly alive to the ways in which society organizes itself along gendered lines. While it is true that from a very early age I was conscious of a deep bodily discomfort – that is, I had an internal sense of anxiety about living my body – this was discovered through living in a world where there was (and perhaps still is) quite rigid expectations of behaviour and dress for those designated 'boy' or 'girl'.

Our society remains structured around what is sometimes called 'gender dimorphism' – that is, clearly defined binary differences between 'men' and women' or 'male' and 'female'. The church both participates in and contributes to our culture's obsession with men and women. One of the creation myths in Genesis says, 'Male and female he created them.' Even if modern science has demonstrated that 'biological sex' is far more complex than many of us ever dreamed, the Bible's claim echoes and has influenced the traditional view – we are either one thing or the other and there is no possibility for change.

When I transitioned at 22 I was not in any

conventional sense a person of faith. Indeed, I was inclined to believe that Christianity represented the forces of stupidity and darkness. My childhood faith – captured in the naïve prayer noted above – had evaporated in the face of disappointment and hard reality. Like many trans (and lesbian, gay, bi and intersex) people I'd grown up to expect only judgment and condemnation from Christians and felt that the safest place for someone like me was to stay as far away from people of faith as possible. My life was complex enough without having to deal with (what I assumed) would be the negativity of people of faith.

Transitioning is, I suggest, one of the toughest things humans can do, even as our society has become more understanding. Because our culture is so defined by an either/or mentality, it struggles with people who are perceived as gender indeterminate. Many trans people themselves have very clear ideas about what gender they are. In my own case, I really struggled during the period in my transition when I was – in terms of visual cues – as much likely to be seen by others as a man as a woman. It is a token of how confident I now feel as a woman that I feel able to play with how I present or 'perform' gender. I feel no need to have long hair or wear girly clothes.

I can play with gender because I'm more at peace with what I am.

I hope that in the twenty plus years since my transition society has embraced gender complexity a little more, but I fear not. As a friend recently told me, when her daughter – who has short hair and prefers gender neutral clothing – went to high school she was constantly asked, 'Are you a boy or a girl?' There remains huge pressure on us to conform and fit into gender stereotypes. Trans people are often accused of living up to and underlining these stereotypes. In my experience, it's more complex. Psychiatrists and therapists often enforce stereotyped behaviour on trans people as a condition of access to things like hormones. Equally, trans people are not a homogenous group – some of us expose and subvert gender norms, others find refuge in them. Trans people, then, are – in that respect – rather like non-trans people.

I came to faith post-transition. In some ways that doesn't surprise me. Jesus said, 'Those who seek to save their life will lose it, and those who lose their life for my sake will save it'. It is a statement with endless resonance. One resonance that many may miss – simply because they've had little cause to question their basic identity – is that in order to lose one's life, one must have one to begin with. That is, to give one's life to God, to lose it, one must have some sense of who one is to begin with. In order to lose oneself there has to be someone there to get lost. In a very important sense, it wasn't until I got into my mid-twenties and I'd worked hard to establish who I was that there was anyone much there to lose. I guess God had been waiting for me to 'appear' for over twenty-five years.

One of the effects of my ruthless attempts to divest myself of 'male-ness' and discover who Rachel was, was that for the first time in my life I felt like I wasn't playing a part. The irony was that the person I had been for over twenty years – shaped and formed in a thousand conventional ways – felt increasingly like a series of masks, a theatrical invention. At the same time, as I 'played' with what it meant to be Rachel (the experiments with clothing, make-up, voice, bodily movement) I felt like I was becoming more myself. In the midst of the creation, the theatre and play, I was becoming a solid person rather than a set of masks.

I'd be lying if I denied that that time – even after the helpful shifts of living full-time as a woman and of changing my name legally to Rachel in 1995 – was one easy march to 'self-realization'. But as I moved into my mid-twenties I felt like I was becoming the person I wanted to be. My life was coming together rather than fragmenting. For the first time I properly had a sense of who I was – hard fought for and hard won, an achievement of self-determination, with little encouragement from others. This was the context for my becoming a Christian.

Since my early teens I had consciously and publicly rejected God. Being an intelligent, status-conscious teen it was evident from an early age that being a Christian was not cool. My family was conventionally religious and it was expected that I be confirmed. I refused and began to cultivate an atheistic image. My advanced education was entirely secular. 'Philosophy' as I was taught to understand it was a secular, hard-nosed matter.

One of the curious things which happened as I became Rachel was an emergent desire to pray. Frankly I found this mostly bewildering and at odds with my life. My life – as a student and teacher of philosophy – was about argument, about thinking, about advancing positions using logic and humour and reasoning. And, yet, forming within me was something more compelling than an argument – a desire or hunger to open myself to something which, my philosophical training suggested, was essentially absurd. It frightened me. Like a person who, because they are a control freak, becomes terrified of what will happen if they let go of their temper, I was frightened about what would happen if I let go. I sensed that if I did so, I might lose myself again. And after fighting so hard to gain a proper sense of myself, surely I would be mad to let that go?

In letting go of myself I had this fear of becoming a drone, a dupe, a kind of faith-driven robot. And this invitation to prayer felt exactly like that: an invitation to let go of control of myself, of my power and self-assurance, of me as the centre of my world. Of me. Having worked so very hard to establish these things in trying circumstances, to feel drawn to let them go was not especially attractive. I had worked so hard to gain a sense of myself and now I felt an invitation to throw that sense into the void. Yet, in finally allowing myself to be in a place where God might 'speak' to me I discovered that rather than being judged, God gave me back myself in new ways. Yes, she challenges me to be faithful to the Living God, but that is by inviting me to be ever more my 'true' self.

Since coming to faith, God has been extraordinarily faithful, even if the Church has often felt a complex and compromised place to be. Given that I was ordained in the Church of England in 2005 you might expect me to be an unalloyed apologist for the Church of England. Yet only a fool would pretend that being trans is seen as ordinary or 'normal' in the Church. While the local church where I serve is supportive and affirming, I am part of an organization where – because I've chosen to be out and unapologetic about who I am - my future job prospects are questionable to say the least. The Church still sees LGBT people as damaged goods.

Many mainline Christian denominations are suspicious of change and challenge. Rather like a high-class hotels their instinct is 'to permit' most things within their 'walls' as long as one is discreet and doesn't cause embarrassment. Perhaps in an era where its reputation has never been more publicly sullied, the Churches are even more anxious about how they measure against rather limited middle-class propriety. Yet God is not especially interested in propriety. She is alive at both the edges of faith and in its broken middle, where she exposes our conventional and comfortable ideas about God to creative renewal.

Should anyone be surprised that being trans is a challenge for the church? This is not simply a matter of what the Bible might or might not have to say about trans people. That trans people remain a problem for the church is one symptom of its ongoing anxieties about gender. To be anything other than the male default is, for the institution, still to be seen as the lesser. Women have known that since the dawn of monotheistic religion.

Yet patriarchal Christianity always holds within itself the seed of its own subversion. That is, it remains a place of hope. For at its centre was, is and always will be the great subversive – Jesus Christ. This is the one who shows us God's authentic faces – Christ does not occupy the positions of power and comfort. He – or as Mother Julian teaches us, 'She' – is the pierced and wounded one. She allows herself to occupy the margins and the mess. She redeems not from a position of power, but from the places where love, hope and reconciliation are being pushed out from the world. The hope for the church lies not with the powerful, but the gloriously alien – the mocked, the strange and the seemingly unlovely with whom Christ stands.

Hilary's story

Hilary Cotton is a white, straight, middle-class, well-educated, able-bodied woman. She lives with her husband in the South-East of England, and they have two fabulous adult children. She has campaigned for women's ordination in the Church of England for over thirty years, as did her mother before her.

I don't remember that being a girl was significant for me when I was young. I was the second of four children – three girls and then a boy – with a university lecturer father and a sociologist mother who went out to work by choice when we were quite small. More important to me was that I was painfully shy, and thin, and very good at maths, all of which seemed to make it hard to fit in socially. Going to an excellent girls' school and a women's college at Oxford confirmed the impression given by my parents that women and men were equally capable, and that having intellectual talent gave a responsibility to contribute to society.

It was only when I started work, in a scientific research organisation, that I was taken aback by some of the ways I was treated by my mainly male colleagues: with a mix of flirtation, caution/suspicion, and patronizing behaviour. I became personally aware that I was in some way a threat, merely for being a young single woman. In church life I had also had good fortune: the local village church buzzed with energy encouraged by a progressive, liberal vicar, who let the small Youth Fellowship lead youth services (attended by long-suffering adults), and invited local evangelists to lead a village mission. I promptly fell in love with Jesus, and though my zeal changed as my passions took a more earthly turn, my sense of the playful, exciting companionship of a male Saviour stayed with me. I remember standing next to my mother, aged about twelve, and hearing her change the words of hymns from 'he' to 'she' and 'him' to 'her', and being embarrassed. But I picked up that for her this was a deeply important issue, and that fact lodged with me.

I soon found that research into sea level was less interesting than the social structures and behavior of colleagues around me, and so I moved into training and development, and loved it. The civil service responded to the

Sex Discrimination Act of 1975 and the Race Relations Act of 1976 with the appointment of Equal Opportunities Officers and mandatory training – which I was asked to work on across the Research Council. We had constant debates about whether we should be changing people's behaviour or attitudes, and whether men and women were different in essence. Handling the discomfort of older men was particularly challenging. They had the kindest of hearts and were keen not to offend women, but found it almost impossible to see them as anything other than the weaker species whom they wanted to protect, and whose real task in life was to run a household and raise children. I am disappointed that I often find that experience repeated in church life even now.

And then I married a vicar. I tussled with whether to change my surname, concluding that I didn't want a 'professional' name and a 'home' name – I am one person – and that in those days it was racy enough for the vicar's wife to be out at work full time, without having a different name from her husband as well. I'm still not sure it was a good decision for us. The comment that throws me, and people still say it, is 'you are so lucky that he irons his own shirts'. Explaining the power of that one sentence to undermine women would take another chapter, so if you don't get it, then find someone who does, and learn!

By now I had left the civil service but an opportunity was offered to return, freelance, as a tutor on a women's development event – a flagship programme bringing together issues of confidence, assertiveness, power, politics, the significance of impression management, and career planning. So by God's accident I found myself working in an arena with other passionate professional 'sisters', many of whom remain firm friends. The work we did, and that I now do for clergywomen, was and is inspiring and healing, and generates courage, respect and confidence where women had not realized how the systems of patriarchy undermine them at a fundamental level.

When did I start to get angry with the church? I think it was when the Act of Synod was forced upon the Church of England General Synod in 1993 This Act made additional concessions to opponents of women's ordination: General Synod had previously rejected all of these concessions, but suddenly they became part of the settlement. I had played a part locally in campaigning for women to be priests, and was exultant when the vote went through in November 1992, assuming that the deed was done. The sense of betrayal when bishops caved in to the opponents, setting up a separate system for those who didn't want female priests anywhere near them, was deeply troubling. We had thought the Church of England had said 'yes'. Now we realized that it had actually said 'Oh, all right then, as long as nobody minds'. The freedom of women to use their gifts for God is still seen as a problem to be handled, not a source of new possibilities to be welcomed and rejoiced in. I often come back to the question 'Why is sexism not seen by the Church of England as the evil that racism is?'. That is the power of patriarchy at work.

Twenty years have passed, during which I have spent much of my time and energy pushing for change. The Church of England is alive with women and men who 'get it' about women, but it takes a long time and a lot of hard spiritual work to get to that place. What does 'getting it' mean, to me? It means that when God is always, always talked of as male then women struggle to know that they are made in God's image, with the closeness and sense of true, freeing identity that brings. That the way the story of Eve is used means that women live with a sense of being, in essence, bad. That the call to humble self-sacrificial living is appropriate for men, who hold power, but not for women, for whom salvation actually means standing tall, speaking up, and refusing to be downtrodden any more. That gender is an issue for men as well as women.

I can highlight some key moments on my own journey:

- Seeing a woman in a dog-collar for the first time and being shocked by how physical my reaction was: feeling a visceral sense of 'No', rather than 'Yes', and having to work out why that was, and what it said about how I really viewed women's place in the Church.
- Realising that in most churches the only images of women are of Mary. No wonder I was beginning to feel an outsider: plenty of portrayals of Father God, Jesus, male disciples, male saints, and even a Holy Dove. But the only one like me was a virgin and a strange mixture of submissive, obedient and idolized, none of which I could identify with.
- Hearing Bishop Cate Waynick of Indianapolis say that opponents of women's ordination are trying just as hard as we are to be faithful. That comment got me over the hatred I couldn't stop myself feeling towards individuals in the church who behaved dismissively towards women.

- Getting over the awkwardness of calling God 'she' and realizing how much that freed my spirit – far more than I could have imagined. To have God as my sister, girl friend, mother, aunt, brought into play all the wonderful women who had been my mentors, and their Godlike-ness as my companions in faith.

- At last, doing some feminist theology with Nicola Slee and brilliant companions: having frameworks for my clumsy thinking about what it means to be a feminist Christian woman, discovering again the importance of our bodies in spiritual experience, and being allowed – allowed – to say outrageous things about God and faith and the Church not only without censure but without having to deal with other people's anxiety, or fear, or it being suggested that I shouldn't think that, or that others will pray for me.

The gap between my own understanding of the Christian faith and the paternalistic Church of England in its institutional ways is pretty big now. Why do I stay? Because I love my local church, with its attempts to be more feminist and still keep everyone flourishing. I have deep friendships there and am proud of the generous welcome we aim to give to anyone, and that we are a thinking, challenging, hopeful church. And a wise friend gave me quote, 'Those who serve the church most are they who ask on a daily basis whether for Christ's sake they should leave it.' I cling on, hoping that God is to be found inside the Church as much as I find her outside, wherever there is goodness and kindness, justice and beauty.

I am currently Chair of WATCH (Women and the Church) where I find like minds and hearts in abundance, and they help me keep faithful to the Church as well as to God. Working with WATCH has brought out unexpected gifts: I have discovered how good my civil service training was in writing briefings, and forensically examining General Synod reports for slippery wording, omissions, and nuances that would undermine the full inclusion of women. I have loved working with Parliamentary colleagues, seeing them convert conversations and briefings into wise and well-crafted political speeches. But I have been dismayed to see so many bright-eyed female clergy become trashed by the labour of running declining parishes and living out a role still defined by expectations of man-with-wife-at-home.

What must we do about gender and the

church? We have to truly pay attention to those who are not male, and listen to their experience, yearnings, ways of being faithful, and ways of learning God. We have to break the mould of the language we use about God and re-kiln it in words and symbols that bring hope, acceptance and glimpses of glory to all our lives. We have to search the tapestries of the history of the church to draw out the threads of holy women and creative communities, of earthly holiness and heaven in ordinary, to affirm the body of Christ is actually a body and not a mind-space or ethereal and spiritual place, separate from everyday activities.

I hope that my grandchildren will grow up in a church where God is fully gendered. Where Jesus is male and the Christa is female and the Creator is female or male or intersex and Christ may return in the form of a woman and the Spirit is a wild mother eagle and a soft male dove and wind and fire and breath, and Wisdom and Word are strong and silent and loving and like thunder. I hope there will be fewer words in worship and more action; that there will be circles not rows, that we will look at each other and listen and sing and weep and laugh.

For a few years in our parish we had a monthly WorshipSpace event, where we gathered to worship differently. We created the hour ourselves, using Iona and Taizé words and music, dancing, drawing, building cairns, holding a silent Eucharist, using cloths and stars and mops and angels to surprise ourselves with aspects of God we had not noticed before. In the 1980s there was a similar burgeoning of writing, thinking, exploring, worshipping alongside mainstream worship in the Church of England, mainly created by women. Since women were ordained as priests I have noticed that the church has swallowed them up and they have, not through their own fault, become priests in a male church. A colleague said to me recently that she thought the church ordains people so they won't be dangerous anymore. But I want more dangerous women, and men, so that we will create a more truly inclusive church. And for that I volunteer.

David's story

David Monteith has been Dean of
Leicester since 2013, supporting a team
of women and men working in a diocese
with a multi-cultural city and rolling English
countryside. This has included re-interring
King Richard III. David previously served
as Team Rector in South Wimbledon
and Associate Vicar at St Martin-in-
the-Fields, London.

I have been reflecting on when it was that I became conscious that I was a boy and that there were other people in the world who were different and called girls. I was the oldest and had a brother and sister with another sister to follow later. I think it was when I started primary school and learnt that there were different toilets supplied for each group with a different logo to represent each. Even then I wondered why boys were represented by trousers and girls by skirts because my sister certainly wore trousers even if I and my brother didn't wear skirts. I presume I knew

before this time that there was difference in
gender but this is my conscious memory of
not only recognising the differentiation but a
recognition that such difference led to further
different physical, cultural, and relational
experience. It was only when I was a mature
adult that I realised there were yet others
in the world who did not sit easily with this
bi-gendered description of human beings. For
example, transgender was not even a phrase I
knew, yet alone understood.

My growing up during the 1970s and 80s
in Northern Ireland was not especially aware
of the politics or theology of gender. Both my
parents worked and indeed my mother was
the more significant bread-winner in our
household. My brother and sisters were treated
in an even way yet we were also significantly
impacted by other cultural factors. The context
of conflict meant that those external to my
community were the focus of threat and the
locus of profound difference. The so-called
normal differences granted by virtue of gender
were of a different order to the more pressing
context of religious and political matters. But
even then as a teenager, I began to notice
distinct cultural differences between a Catholic
and Protestant community relating to human
embodied identity.

One of these certainly related to gender and was seen at its most profound when there was a funeral. It was mainly women and girls who occupied the realm of the private and domestic whilst men occupied the public sphere. So my mum might have visited a local bereaved family at home but my dad would go to the funeral. But during 'the Troubles' many funerals became public in the media. I noticed that at big Roman Catholic funerals many women were also present. If there was also an aspect of political protest at such funerals then much of this was also voiced by women. All this was in stark contrast to Protestant funerals marked by rows of men in heavy black overcoats. I could see that gender was a key shaper of identity, role and culture.

For me this was further reinforced in church which again was public sphere and so populated by men. The clergy, church wardens and lay leadership were nearly all men with the occasional exception such as a local GP who by virtue of her other standing in the community as a skilled person, enabled her to take her place in church leadership. All this was in contrast to my teenage years of spiritual development when as part of youth groups; I encountered a community of participation involving young men and women which looked very different to my usual experience of church. This youth world was largely lay-led and had strong bonds of affection, a sense of mutuality of care and a common sense of learning and cohesive identity. Naturally, given it was made up of teenagers, there was a hormonal undercurrent with an awareness of gender being primarily connected with attraction and sexuality. But here was a space where gender was part of the equation but where leadership was shared between us and where gender did not determine role or place in our groups.

I then went off to university in Durham, to read zoology. There I encountered a very different culture which was embedded in the life and politics of the church since half of my college trained people to be ordained. Many of my friends were reading theology even if I escaped to the science site. I got involved with the College Chapel and the Christian Union. Within a very short time I came to understand that gender was a huge issue in the church as I encountered the debates about the ordination of women to the priesthood.

My youth group experience of mutual spiritual leadership made me very suspicious of those arguing against the change in the wider church. I had experienced life where existing patterns had been reworked so I couldn't quite see how that could not be more widely so. I was meeting for the first time women training for ordained ministry – at that stage diaconal service but there was growing hope of priesthood and episcopacy and before I could logically articulate why this might be right, I knew it to be so.

Equally, I began to become more aware of myself now away from family and away from what I could now see was quite a constrained social culture. So I had to face my own gendered identity more. I saw how conflict or some other more immediate presenting issue can mask aspects of humanity or relegate them as being secondary. This exerted an oppressive impact. Later in life when I found myself visiting South Africa regularly, especially to communities of rural poor people, I would see again how in this case the presenting issues of poverty and HIV/AIDS masked the profound issues of domestic violence and sexual violence against women. Issues of gender and in particular issues of justice for women are sometimes too hard to face and become conveniently ignored.

So away from the constraints of Northern Ireland my horizons broadened further. For example, I met gay men and women knowingly for the first time. This was very unsettling because of the newness of the experience. Now not only had I to work out that men and women might be different but that different men and women might carry their sense of what it was to be male or female in very different ways because that was also filtered through sexuality or ethnicity or social class.

All this learning was never academic for me but very close to home as it helped to challenge and interpret my own growing sense of self. These realities would be played out in local politics when 'town and gown' encountered one another. I read about the gendered politics of poverty and economic injustice in the North East and I saw that played out through typical 1980s student politics too. It was after all Durham in the years following the miners' strike. There had to be a reckoning with myself and an attempt at integration of the fragments, incorporating what I had been learning about being a man and what I had been learning from others about being women. I was much more aware of the sin of sexism, recognising how I had been conditioned by it. This was further complicated by my emerging identity as gay. I met regressive as well as progressive voices. I saw how some gay men could help me grow into a way of being a man which made for safe and enriching relationships with women. Whilst others often full of their own self-loathing led to distorted views of women and destructive versions of masculinity. So what parts of my inherited experience of maleness needed to endure? Must I conform to the patterns of gay maleness that I was witnessing? Was there a way to be simply me? Could I have confidence as a man whilst remaining aware of the need to keep learning?

I was ordained Deacon in 1993 and priest in 1994. This means that my cohort of students was the first group of men and women who might have been ordained together. Nearly everyone at my theological college believed in the ordination of women to the priesthood with a variety of degree of commitment to making this change. Those days at theological college were tense and I went with a group to be outside Church House as the final debates about the ordination of women took place. None of us really contemplated what a 'No' would mean yet we all knew that the need to receive a two-thirds majority in all three sections of the Synod was a high bar. I had voiced to my ordaining bishop the possibility of me remaining a deacon and not being priested if the vote had not gone through so to be visibly in solidarity with my female colleagues. I did not feel comfortable at that stage being an ordained representative of an institutionally sexist church. As things worked out, the vote went through, women were ordained and my cohort of ordinary women and men curates set the scene for the future trajectory of the ordained life of the church. This means that in my ordained life I have always worked with male and female colleagues. This does not mean necessarily that the work of understanding the place and experience of gender has advanced massively. If anything, because there has been progress there is a tendency to think 'we've done that'. This has only really become clearer to me since becoming a Dean at the time when at last the ordination of women to the episcopate has been decided.

I sit on a Bishop's staff; I attend the national meetings of Deans; I attend synods and many other church groups. It is nearly always the case that men remain in the majority despite women being the majority 'in the pews'. Many of my female colleagues have found part-time roles or work in chaplaincy. In my diocese there are still few women as vicars of major parishes or teams. There is some awareness to try and redress this but it is slow. So recently when appointing a new Residentiary Canon we tried to shape our advert and paperwork in ways that would attract lots of people including able women. The embedded assumptions derived from our different experiences as men and women still need naming and exploring. Often they can implicitly exclude others or impede the kind of new full humanity dreamt of in the gospel. They need redemption. This means unlearning followed by new learning which invariably has to be intentional.

So I recognise that the particular experience of gender which I personally bring shapes my behaviour and thought patterns. I recognise that my background has shaped me and I can feel that I am not really conforming to what is expected of a 'real man'. As a Dean you have to be very connected with the institutional life of community and these worlds are still relearning how to relate to contemporary culture. I am not a sportsman. I don't shoot or hunt. I have no military background. I did not go to a private school. I do not have any children. I do not have a wife. I try to create consensus rather than alpha-male decisiveness. Many of these things are still associated with what it is to be a man in public church leadership. This is not a space I can fill and so I find myself quietly trying to re-invent the expectations of role. Some women also share a similar experience where their approach does not fit and is not valued or even rejected. The temptation for collusion or just the sheer pressure of busy demanding lives means that a lazy unchallenged acceptance can become the lowest common denominator and so gender myths are perpetuated.

However, at least being part of church and repeatedly being called back to Jesus Christ's vision for a new kind of community means that unexamined gender assumptions will simply not remain settled. His portrayal as a man with what I see as non-discriminatory vision remains enticing and convicting for me. As women become bishops, potentially we enter the next stage of mutual learning about what it may mean to become more human in the particularity of our own gender.

Natalie's story

*Natalie Collins is a Gender Justice
Specialist. She works to enable individuals
and organisations to prevent and respond
to male violence against women. She is
also the Creator of DAY an innovative youth
domestic abuse and exploitation education
programme. She speaks and writes on
understanding and ending
gender injustice.*

I've been part of the church my whole life. I was born into it. I mean, my mother did not actually birth me into a pew or anything; I was born in a hospital, on a Sunday. One of the first things my dad did was drive to the Sunday evening service, run down the aisle and announce, 'It's a girl! We've called her Natalie Joy!'

I doubt anyone in church on that Sunday 19 August 1984 thought 'Well that's unfortunate! Girls don't do too well in society or in the church.' The vote had been won for women many decades previous and four years before my birth women were even afforded the right within law to apply for a loan or credit without their husband's permission. Yet it would be another decade before the Church of England included women in the priesthood and the reality of domestic and sexual violence for women and girls across the UK and globally was being talked about mainly by a few brave women who opened their homes and lives to the broken and the hurting.

I wasn't raised to think much about being a girl. My parents weren't happy for either my brother or I to play with guns. We were given the same opportunities. I found out recently that my dad won a 'New Man of the Nineties' award for representing the less macho, more cerebral aspects of masculinity that were seen as new in the early nineties. Even so my parents fulfilled traditional gender roles, with my mum being the main carer and my dad the main wage earner. I never saw my gender as a thing really. I knew I was female, but didn't begin puberty until I was well into my teens. My lack of womanly curves and my penchant for climbing trees coupled with living at least twenty years before the extreme level of gender stereotyping in children's clothes and toys we see today left me in the main part oblivious of there being many gender differences, except the obvious of whether someone's genitals went inwards or outwards. It wasn't until I reached my late teens that my being female led to life altering consequences.

I was seventeen years old when I met Seth[1] through a friend. He was charming, beautiful and articulate. My friend had told me that he had recently become a Christian thereby fulfilling the single most important aspect of my Christian relationship education; make sure any potential romantic interest was washed in the blood (or as most of the world would describe it, had become a Christian). Very quickly the relationship became extremely intense; he wanted to be with me every waking moment, quickly encouraging me to do things I was not allowed to and that went against my values and my faith. I was a passionate evangelist in my youth. I loved Jesus and proudly declared my virgin status in my first week of college. As would only be proper I had explained my virgin status to Seth and had shared my passion for Jesus. Within days he had dragged all my secrets out of me and shared his damaged life with me. Weeks into the relationship he sat me down and told me he would hurt me and therefore I should end the relationship. The healthy person's response to this would be,

---

[1] Name has been changed.

'This person is clearly dangerous. Maintain eye contact, smile and walk ... Away ... Slowly.' My reaction was less of that and more of thinking, 'Jesus can save him! I can bring the truth of the Gospel to him. Isn't it wonderful that he's being so honest?! That's the first step towards repentance!'

Within less than two weeks of meeting him Seth had manipulated me into having sex with him. That this was not a consensual choice I made to have sex before marriage, but rather sexual abuse would take me over five years to fully understand and accept. I had learnt that sex was really the same as marriage and so concluded that at seventeen, having been sexually abused, that I should accept that this meant I was essentially married to Seth and must commit to him for the rest of my life. I had known him twelve days. Seth's words became less kind, his insults towards me grew steadily more offensive. Sex with other girls and empty apologies were his weekly routine and I was trapped; sure that this was my life forever. I was committed to being Jesus to him; forgiving him whatever he did and trying to forget it, being kind and loving to him no matter how deeply his words wounded me. He wouldn't let me use contraception. His views alongside a Catholic education left me unable

47

to control my own fertility and so the evening of my eighteenth birthday was spent telling gathered family members that I was pregnant.

What ensued was the worst three years of my life. Seth controlled and manipulated every aspect of my life. My pregnancy was characterised by kidney infections, exhaustion and pain as he refused to work or help me with household chores; my parents' traditional gender roles contributing to my view that this wasn't a big deal. His on-going affairs eroded my trust and left me on constant high alert. My daughter was a light within the darkness of that time and on the days when I felt I couldn't keep going; her life gave me a reason to continue trudging on. Three months after her birth Seth and I got married; I thought that was the way to best honour God within the midst of what I saw as my bad choices. Seth raped me, told me I was worthless and useless, exhausted me and on occasions left me suicidal. He lied to me and intentionally isolated me from my friends and family. He would push me to do things that he knew were against my value system, wearing me down until I gave in to his demands. He would laugh at me, humiliate and degrade me. By the time we were both nineteen years old he had been convicted of sex offences against teenage girls. He said he was sorry and I thought forgiveness meant wiping the slate clean. From then on I also experienced abuse from neighbours for being married to a registered sex offender. I tried to maintain my faith in God but maintaining a relationship with an abuser and with God proved impossible. After his conviction Seth was banned from my church due to child protection concerns. Though it had become apparent early in the relationship he wasn't actually committed to Jesus, the church's decision isolated me even further.

Often people ask of those who have experienced abuse, 'Why didn't you just leave?' My questions to such people; 'Why is your focus on the person being hurt? Why not ask why doesn't he just stop?' Until such time where every person begins asking questions of the perpetrator and not of the person experiencing the abuse, there will not be real change. I couldn't leave. I was depressed, desolate, isolated and controlled. He spent all our money and refused to take any responsibility. I was stuck. I would still be there now if it wasn't for circumstances far beyond my control. At twenty I became pregnant with my son. I began distancing myself from Seth and trying to find a way out. So he raped me.

People misunderstand sexual violence.

They consider it to be a destructive form of uncontrollable lust, of twisted sexual desire. In fact, rape is not about sex at all. It is about destruction and control. It breaks the soul of every human being subjected to it. It is a choice and rather than a result of lost control, it is the very essence of control; controlling and decimating another human being.

My son was born three months premature. He was placed in a hospital fifty miles away. My daughter and I lived in hospital with him and it was this that enabled me to separate successfully from Seth. I was forced to leave. It was a long and often painful journey to see my son become healthy. He was in hospital for five months and needed specialist care until after he was a year old. There is much to be told about the journey I embarked on after becoming free from Seth; there is not the space to share it here.

Seven years ago I remarried. My husband Andrew has supported me through depression, Post Traumatic Stress Disorder, a family court case and the on-going impact of what I was subjected to. He has inherited two of the most wonderful children in all the world (I may be biased in saying that ...) and has at various times been a full-time wage earner and a full-time dad in order to support me as we have walked in God's call for our lives.

One of the struggles I worked through was the question of why. Why did Seth hurt me? Was it my fault? How could someone do that to another human being? The answer, I found, lies fundamentally in my being female. He chose to hurt me because he believed that he owned me and was therefore entitled to behave in the ways he did. Those beliefs of ownership and entitlement are rooted in the patriarchal culture that we all find ourselves living in. What happened to me was horrific, but on a structural level is merely the logical conclusion of a global system in which men are unfairly advantaged over women; in which male privilege taints every human interaction globally. It is not that men cannot experience violence or abuse nor that women are not capable of evil behaviour, but rather the current system disadvantages women-as-a-class and advantages men-as-a-class. Gender stereotyping, rigid gender roles, the sexualisation and objectification of women and childhood, the reducing of women's and girls' bodies to a product to be consumed sit at one end of the spectrum of oppression that women-as-a-class face. At the other end of the spectrum sit female genital mutilation, female infanticide, so-called honour based violence and rape as a weapon of war used to terrorise women worldwide. Men are the majority holders of power in every society globally even though women form 51% of the global population. None of this is a coincidence; it is the reality of patriarchy.

In Genesis 3:16 we discover that patriarchy is a primary consequence of The Fall, alongside childbirth and hard labour for little result. Patriarchy is not an accident or a conspiracy theory, it is a principality and power as old as sin itself. Yet, as Christians we know that in Jesus we find fullness of life and freedom from sin. As such it would be logical to assume that the Church would be free from patriarchy, that our community would be one in which women have equal power with men and in which a prophetic message of liberation for women would be preached from every pulpit. However this is not the church we see. My experiences growing up in church left me ill-equipped to form healthy relationships. Forgiveness became a weapon of collusion and denial, rather than the tool of liberation and freedom I have discovered it can be. Traditional understandings of headship, submission, gender and sex contributed to my inability to escape Seth. As the people of God, we must awaken to the spiritual battle raging around us and within our community and our very souls.

I have made it through. I am blessed to be able to work full time on ending violence against women and addressing gender injustice. I have the amazing privilege of hearing so many stories of brokenness and restoration and of being able to give all that I am to Jesus in the hope that He will use me to bring glory to Him, to bring this good news of freedom to those who need to hear it, to support the broken hearted in healing and working with the Holy Spirit in setting the captives free. This call is not just mine, it is for each of us who have given ourselves to Jesus; what is the part God is calling you to?

PART 2

The rise and fall of Default Man

GRAYSON PERRY

GRAYSON PERRY is a Turner Prize-winning artist. In 2012, his series *All In The Best Possible Taste* was broadcast on Channel 4, and in 2013 he delivered the BBC's Reith Lectures. The article 'The Rise and Fall of Default Man' first appeared in the *New Statesman*, 8 October 2014. It is reprinted here by permission. The article is referred to in both the Theology and Resources section of this book.

Paddle your canoe up the River Thames and you will come round the bend and see a forest of huge totems jutting into the sky. Great shiny monoliths in various phallic shapes, they are the wondrous cultural artefacts of a remarkable tribe. We all know someone from this powerful tribe but we very rarely, if ever, ascribe their power to the fact that they have a particular tribal identity.

I think this tribe, a small minority of our native population, needs closer examination. In the UK, its members probably make up about 10 per cent of the population; globally, probably less than 1 per cent. In a phrase used more often in association with Operation Yewtree, they are among us and hide in plain sight.

They dominate the upper echelons of our society, imposing, unconsciously or otherwise, their values and preferences on the rest of the population. With their colourful textile phalluses hanging round their necks, they make up an overwhelming majority in government, in boardrooms and also in the media.

They are, of course, white, middle-class, heterosexual men, usually middle-aged. And

every component of that description has historically played a part in making this tribe a group
that punches far, far above its weight. I have
struggled to find a name for this identity that
will trip off the tongue, or that doesn't clutter the
page with unpronounceable acronyms such as
WMCMAHM. 'The White Blob' was a strong con-
tender but in the end I opted to call him Default
Man. I like the word 'default', for not only does it
mean 'the result of not making an active choice',
but two of its synonyms are 'failure to pay' and
'evasion', which seems incredibly appropriate,
considering the group I wish to talk about.

Today, in politically correct 21st-century
Britain, you might think things would have
changed but somehow the Great White Male
has thrived and continues to colonise the high-
status, high-earning, high-power roles (93
per cent of executive directors in the UK are
white men; 77 per cent of parliament is male).
The Great White Male's combination of good
education, manners, charm, confidence and
sexual attractiveness (or 'money', as I like to
call it) means he has a strong grip on the keys to
power. Of course, the main reason he has those
qualities in the first place is what he is, not
what he has achieved. John Scalzi, in his blog
Whatever, thought that being a straight white
male was like playing the computer game called

Life with the difficulty setting on 'Easy'. If you are a Default Man you look like power.

I must confess that I qualify in many ways to be a Default Man myself but I feel that by coming from a working-class background and being an artist and a transvestite, I have enough cultural distance from the towers of power. I have space to turn round and get a fairly good look at the edifice.

In the course of making my documentary series about identity, *Who Are You?*, for Channel 4, the identity I found hardest to talk about, the most elusive, was Default Man's. Somehow, his world-view, his take on society, now so overlaps with the dominant narrative that it is like a Death Star hiding behind the moon. We cannot unpick his thoughts and feelings from the 'proper, right-thinking' attitudes of our society. It is like in the past, when people who spoke in cut-glass, RP, BBC tones would insist they did not have an accent, only northerners and poor people had one of those. We live and breathe in a Default Male world: no wonder he succeeds, for much of our society operates on his terms.

Chris Huhne (60, Westminster, PPE Magdalen, self-destructively heterosexual), the Default Man we chose to interview for our series, pooh-poohed any suggestion when asked if he benefited from membership or if he represented this group. Lone Default Man will never admit to, or be fully aware of, the tribal advantages of his identity. They are, naturally, full subscribers to that glorious capitalist project, they are *individuals*!

This adherence to being individuals is the nub of the matter. Being 'individual' means that if they achieve something good, it is down to their own efforts. They got the job because they are brilliant, not because they are a Default Man, and they are also presumed more competent by other Default Men. If they do something bad it is also down to the individual and not to do with their gender, race or class. If a Default Man commits a crime it is not because fraud or sexual harassment, say, are endemic in his tribe (coughs), it is because he is a wrong 'un. If a Default Man gets emotional it is because he is a 'passionate' individual, whereas if he were a woman it would often be blamed on her sex.

When we talk of identity, we often think of groups such as black Muslim lesbians in wheelchairs. This is because identity only seems to become an issue when it is challenged or under threat. Our classic Default Man is rarely under existential threat; consequently, his identity remains unexamined. It ambles along blithely, never having to stand up for its rights or to defend its homeland.

When talking about identity groups, the word 'community' often crops up. The working class, gay people, black people or Muslims are always represented by a 'community leader'. We rarely, if ever, hear of the white middle-class community. 'Communities' are defined in the eye of Default Man. Community seems to be a euphemism for the vulnerable lower orders. Community is 'other'. Communities usually seem to be embattled, separate from society. 'Society' is what Default Man belongs to.

In news stories such as the alleged 'Trojan Horse' plot in Birmingham schools and the recent child-abuse scandal in Rotherham, the central involvement of an ethnic or faith 'community' skews the attitudes of police, social services and the media. The Muslim or Pakistani heritage of those accused becomes the focus. I'm not saying that faith and ethnic groups don't have their particular problems but the recipe for such trouble is made up of more than one spicy, foreign ingredient. I would say it involves more than a few handfuls of common-or-garden education/class issues, poor mental health and, of course, the essential ingredient in nearly all nasty or violent problems, men. Yeah, men – bit like them Default Men but without suits on.

In her essay 'Visual Pleasure and Narrative Cinema', published in 1975, Laura Mulvey coined the term 'the male gaze'. She was writing about how the gaze of the movie camera reflected the heterosexual male viewpoint of the directors (a viewpoint very much still with us, considering that only 9 per cent of the top 250 Hollywood films in 2012 were directed by women and only 2 per cent of the cinematographers were female).

The Default Male gaze does not just dominate cinema, it looks down on society like the eye on Sauron's tower in *The Lord of the Rings*. Every other identity group is 'othered' by it. It is the gaze of the expensively nondescript corporate leader watching consumers adorn themselves with his company's products the better to get his attention.

Default Man feels he is the reference point from which all other values and cultures are judged. Default Man is the zero longitude of identities.

He has forged a society very much in his own image, to the point where now much of what other groups think and feel is the same. They take on the attitudes of Default Man because they are the attitudes of our elders, our education, our government, our media. If Default Men approve of something it must be good, and if they disapprove it must be bad, so people end up hating themselves, because their internalised Default Man is berating them for being female, gay, black, silly or wild.

I often hear women approvingly describe themselves or other women as feisty. Feisty, I feel, has sexist implications, as if standing up for yourself was exceptional in a woman. It sounds like a word that a raffish Lothario would use about a difficult conquest.

I once gave a talk on kinky sex and during the questions afterwards a gay woman floated an interesting thought: 'Is the legalising of gay marriage an attempt to neutralise the otherness of homosexuals?' she asked. Was the subversive alternative being neutered by allowing gays to marry and ape a hetero lifestyle? Many gay people might have enjoyed their dangerous outsider status. Had Default Man implanted a desire to be just like him?

Is the fact that we think like Default Man the reason why a black female Doctor Who has not happened, that it might seem 'wrong' or clunky? In my experience, when I go to the doctor I am more likely to see a non-white woman than a Default Man.

It is difficult to tweezer out the effect of

Default Man on our culture, so ingrained is it after centuries of their rules. A friend was once on a flight from Egypt. As it came in to land at Heathrow he looked down at the rows of mock-Tudor stockbroker-belt houses in west London. Pointing them out, he said to the Egyptian man sitting next to him: 'Oh well, back to boring old England.' The Egyptian replied, 'Ah, but to me this is very exotic.' And he was right. To much of the world the Default Englishman is a funny foreign folk icon, with his bowler hat, his Savile Row suit and Hugh Grant accent, living like Reggie Perrin in one of those polite suburban semis. All the same, his tribal costume and rituals have probably clothed and informed the global power elite more than any other culture. Leaders wear his clothes, talk his language and subscribe to some version of his model of how society 'should be'.

When I was at art college in the late Seventies/early Eighties, one of the slogans the feminists used was: 'Objectivity is Male Subjectivity.' This brilliantly encapsulates how male power nestles in our very language, exerting influence at the most fundamental level. Men, especially Default Men, have put forward their biased, highly emotional views as somehow 'rational', more considered, more 'calm down, dear'. Women and 'exotic' minorities are framed as 'passionate' or 'emotional' as if they, the Default Men, had this unique ability to somehow look round the side of that most interior lens, the lens that is always distorted by our feelings. Default Man somehow had a dispassionate, empirical, objective vision of the world as a birthright, and everyone else was at the mercy of turbulent, uncontrolled feelings. That, of course, explained why the 'others' often held views that were at such odds with their supposedly cool, analytic vision of the world.

Recently, footage of the UN spokesman Chris Gunness breaking down in tears as he spoke of the horrors occurring in Gaza went viral. It was newsworthy because reporters and such spokespeople are supposed to be dispassionate and impartial. To show such feelings was to be 'unprofessional'. And lo! The inherited mental health issues of Default Man are cast as a necessity for serious employment.

I think Default Man should be made aware of the costs and increasing obsolescence of this trait, celebrated as 'a stiff upper lip'. This habit of denying, recasting or suppressing emotion may give him the veneer of 'professionalism' but, as David Hume put it: 'Reason is a slave of the passions.' To be unaware of or unwilling to examine feelings means those feelings have free rein to influence behaviour unconsciously. Unchecked, they can motivate Default Man covertly, unacknowledged, often wreaking havoc. Even if rooted in long-past events in the deep unconscious, these emotions still fester, churning in the dark at the bottom of the well. Who knows what unconscious, screwed-up 'personal journeys' are being played out on the nation by emotionally illiterate Default Men?

Being male and middle class and being from a generation that still valued the stiff upper lip means our Default Man is an ideal candidate for low emotional awareness. He sits in a gender/class/age nexus marked 'Unexploded Emotional Time Bomb'.

These people have been in charge of our world for a long time.

Things may be changing. Women are often stereotyped as the emotional ones, and men as rational. But, after the 2008 crash, the picture looked different, as Hanna Rosin wrote in an article in the *Atlantic* titled 'The End of Men':

Researchers have started looking into the relationship between testosterone and excessive risk, and wondering if groups of men, in some basic hormonal way, spur each other to make reckless decisions. The picture emerging is a mirror image of the traditional gender map: men and markets on the side of the irrational and overemotional, and women on the side of the cool and level-headed.

Over the centuries, empirical, clear thinking has become branded with the image of Default Men. They were the ones granted the opportunity, the education, the leisure, the power to put their thoughts out into the world. In people's minds, what do professors look like? What do judges look like? What do leaders look like? The very aesthetic of seriousness has been monopolised by Default Man. Practically every person on the globe who wants to be taken seriously in politics, business and the media dresses up in some way like a Default Man, in a grey, western, two-piece business suit. Not for nothing is it referred to as 'power dressing'. We've all seen those photo ops of world leaders: colour and pattern shriek out as anachronistic. Consequently, many women have adopted this armour of the unremarkable. Angela Merkel, the most powerful woman in the world, wears a predictable unfussy, feminised version of the male look. Hillary Clinton has adopted a similar style. Some businesswomen describe this need to tone down their feminine appearance as 'taking on the third gender'.

Peter Jones on *Dragons' Den* was once referred to as 'eccentric' for wearing brightly coloured stripy socks. So rigid is the Default Man look that men's suit fashions pivot on tiny changes of detail at a glacial pace. US politicians wear such a narrow version of the Default Man look that you rarely see one wearing a tie that is not plain or striped.

One tactic that men use to disguise their subjectively restricted clothing choices is the justification of spurious function. As if they need a watch that splits lap times and works 300 feet underwater, or a Himalayan mountaineer's jacket for a walk in the park. The rufty-tufty army/hunter camouflage pattern is now to boys as pink is to girls. Curiously, I think the real function of the sober business suit is not to look smart but as camouflage. A person in a grey suit is invisible, in the way burglars often wear hi-vis jackets to pass as unremarkable 'workmen'. The business suit is the uniform of those who do the looking, the appraising. It rebuffs comment by its sheer ubiquity. Many office workers loathe dress-down Fridays because they can no longer hide behind a suit. They might have to expose something of their messy selves through their 'casual' clothes. Modern, over professionalised politicians, having spent too long in the besuited tribal compound, find casual dress very difficult to get right convincingly. David Cameron, while ruining Converse basketball shoes for the rest of us, never seemed to me as if he belonged in a pair.

When I am out and about in an eye-catching frock, men often remark to me, 'Oh, I wish I could dress like you and did not have to wear a boring suit.' *Have* to! The male role is heavily policed from birth, by parents, peers and bosses. Politicians in particular are harshly kept in line by a media that seems to uphold more bizarrely rigid standards of conformity than those held by any citizen. Each component of the Default Male role – his gender, his class, his age and his sexuality – confines him to an ever narrower set of behaviours, until riding a bicycle or growing a beard, having messy hair or enjoying a pint are seen as ker-azy eccentricity. The fashionable members' club Shoreditch House, the kind of place where 'creatives' with two iPhones and three bicycles hang out, has a 'No Suits' rule. How much of this is a pseudo-rebellious pose and how much is in recognition of the pernicious effect of the overgrown schoolboy's uniform, I do not know.

I dwell on the suit because I feel it exemplifies how the upholders of Default Male values hide in plain sight. Imagine if, by democratic decree, the business suit was banned, like certain items of Islamic dress have been banned in some countries. Default Men would flounder and complain that they were not being treated with 'respect'.

The most pervasive aspect of the Default Man identity is that it masquerades very efficiently as 'normal' – and 'normal', along with 'natural', is a dangerous word, often at the root of hateful prejudice. As Sherrie Bourg Carter, author of *High-Octane Women*, writes: 'Women in today's workforce ... are experiencing a much more camouflaged foe – second-generation gender biases ... "work cultures and practices that appear neutral and natural on their face", yet they reflect masculine values and life situations of men.'

Personally, working in the arts, I do not often encounter Default Man en masse, but when I do it is a shock. I occasionally get invited to formal dinners in the City of London and on arrival, I am met, in my lurid cocktail dress, with a sea of dinner jackets; perhaps harshly, my expectations of a satisfying conversation drop. I feel rude mentioning the black-clad elephant in the room. I sense that I am the anthropologist allowed in to the tribal ritual.

Of course, this weird minority, these curiously dominant white males, are anything but normal. 'Normal,' as Carl Jung said, 'is the ideal aim for the unsuccessful.' They like to keep their abnormal power low-key: the higher the power, the duller the suit and tie, a Mercedes rather than a Rolls, just another old man chatting casually to prime ministers at the wedding of a tabloid editor.

Revolution is happening. I am loath to use the R word because bearded young men usually characterise it as sudden and violent. But that is just another unhelpful cliché. I feel real revolutions happen thoughtfully in peacetime. A move away from the dominance of Default Man is happening, but way too slowly. Such changes in society seem to happen at a pace set by incremental shifts in the animal spirits of the population. I have heard many of the 'rational' (i.e., male) arguments against quotas and positive discrimination but I feel it is a necessary fudge to enable just change to happen in the foreseeable future. At the present rate of change it will take more than a hundred years before the UK parliament is 50 per cent female.

The outcry against positive discrimination

is the wail of someone who is having their privilege taken away. For talented black, female and working-class people to take their just place in the limited seats of power, some of those Default Men are going to have to give up their seats.

Perhaps Default Man needs to step down from some of his most celebrated roles. I'd happily watch a gay black James Bond and an all-female *Top Gear*, *QI* or *Have I Got News for You*. Jeremy Paxman should have been replaced by a woman on *Newsnight*. More importantly, we need a quota of MPs who (shock) have not been to university but have worked on the shop floor of key industries; have had life experiences that reflect their constituents'; who actually represent the country rather than just a narrow idea of what a politician looks like. The ridiculousness of objections to quotas would become clear if you were to suggest that, instead of calling it affirmative action, we adopted 'Proportionate Default Man Quotas' for government and business. We are wasting talent. Women make up a majority of graduates in such relevant fields as law.

Default Man seems to be the embodiment of George Bernard Shaw's unreasonable man: 'The reasonable man adapts himself to the world; the unreasonable one persists in trying to make the world adapt to himself. Therefore all progress depends on the unreasonable man.' Default Man's days may be numbered; a lot of his habits are seen at best as old-fashioned or quaint and at worst as redundant, dangerous or criminal. He carries a raft of unhelpful habits and attitudes gifted to him from history – adrenalin addiction, a need for certainty, snobbery, emotional constipation and an overdeveloped sense of entitlement – which have often proved disastrous for society and can also stop poor Default Man from leading a fulfilling life.

Earlier this year, at the Being A Man festival at the Southbank Centre in London, I gave a talk on masculinity called: 'Men, Sit Down for your Rights!'. A jokey title, yes, but one making a serious point: that perhaps, if men were to loosen their grip on power, there might be some benefits for them. The straitjacket of the Default Man identity is not necessarily one happily donned by all members of the tribe: many struggle with the bad fit of being leader, provider, status hunter, sexual predator, respectable and dignified symbol of straight achievement. Maybe the 'invisible weightless backpack' that the US feminist Peggy McIntosh uses to describe white privilege, full of 'special provisions, maps, passports, codebooks, visas, clothes, tools and blank checks', does weigh rather a lot after all.

PART 3

Theology

A Theology of Gender
ROSEMARY LAIN-PRIESTLEY

*Each book in this series contains a
substantial theological reflection by
an expert in the field. Here Rosemary
Lain-Priestley helps us explore what
it may mean to be part of an inclusive
church where women and men can
explore and express their 'gendered
experience of the world'.*

ROSEMARY LAIN-PRIESTLEY is an Anglican priest and currently Dean of Women's
Ministry in the Diocese of London. She has
been Associate Vicar of St Martin-in-the-Fields
and a contributor to BBC Radio 4's 'Thought
for the Day', and is author of *The Courage to
Connect, Unwrapping the Sacred* and *Does My
Soul Look Big in This?*

CHAPTER 1

Why are we still talking about gender?

The gender balance

In *The End of Men: And the Rise of Women,* the American journalist Hanna Rosin argues that in a number of countries in both the Global North and South women are now ahead of men in education and the workplace, combining their achievements with domestic happiness. Men, she warns, have been disproportionately affected by economic recession and are feeling marginalised, struggling to find a new identity. United Nations figures paint a markedly different picture: women comprise half the world's population yet number 70% of those who live in poverty; they do 75% of the world's agricultural work whilst owning only 1% of the land; they represent only 20% of the world's parliamentarians.[2] Closer to home, in a typical

[2] *Of the Same Flesh: Exploring a Theology of Gender* by Christian Aid, p. 6. Quoting United Nations data.

month in 2011 in the UK, '78% of newspaper articles were written by men and 84% of reporters and guests on Radio 4's Today show were men',[3] and in 2014 there were 10,000 reports of sexism logged via the online 'Everyday Sexism Project'[4]. Yet men are disproportionately impacted by alcoholism and suicide, and far less likely to seek help for mental health issues. Grayson Perry, the artist and social commentator writing in the *New Statesman (reprinted in this book, pp. 57–74)* speaks of 'Default Man' (who is straight, white and middle-class), 'The straitjacket of the Default Man identity is not necessarily one happily donned by all members of the tribe: many struggle with the bad fit of being leader, provider, status hunter, sexual predator, respectable and dignified symbol of straight achievement.'[5] Rosin may well be right in identifying that some men are restless and discontented, asking questions about their roles and identity.

But what is gender?

It seems that gender issues are alive, well and controversial. But what exactly do we mean

---

[3] Kira Cochrane, *Guardian,* 4 December 2011.

[4] www.everydaysexism.com

[5] Grayson Perry, 'The Rise and Fall of Default Man', *New Statesman*, 8 October 2014.

by gender? For clarity we need a definition of terms, which the World Health Organisation helpfully provides:

> 'Sex refers to the biological and physiological characteristics that define men and women. Gender refers to the socially constructed roles, behaviours, activities, and attributes that a given society considers appropriate for men and women ... Male and female are sex categories, while *masculine and feminine are gender categories.*' [6]

Sex has not always been understood as clearly binary. Hippocrates (c460-c370 BCE) saw male and female as being on a continuum, with hermaphrodites in the middle; Galen (AD 129–c216) thought that there was one single sex: women being a version of men with inverse reproductive organs. The writings of some of the Early Church Fathers, perhaps especially Tertullian and Augustine, reflect this latter perspective: they seem to consider woman to be an incomplete form of man! This goes some way to explaining the deep-seated cultural prejudices which have distorted gender

[6] World Health Organisation website http://www.who.int/gender/whatisgender/en/

relationships in many periods of Christian history.

Male and female in God's image

Such prejudices, however, do not accord with the two accounts of Creation found in Genesis chapters 1–2. The first tells us that on the sixth day: 'God created humankind in his image, in the image of God he created them; male and female he created them' (Genesis 1:27). The word used for humankind is *ādām* and both male and female reflect God's image. In the other account, in Genesis 2, God forms Adam (*ādām*) from the dust of the ground and breathes life into him, then decides that he should not be alone, and forms Eve from Adam's side. The two are of exactly the same substance, differentiated at this point as *īss* and *īssa*. Their task of nurturing the earth is to be shared, with no apportioning of different roles. A theology of gender for the church today will be about exploring the sense in which women and men are the same and also our 'otherness', as we are differentiated biologically and it would seem logical that there might be other differences too.

Venus and Mars, or the same planet?

In *Delusions of Gender*, the psychologist Cordelia Fine challenges the idea proffered by some neuroscientists that women and men have brains that are wired differently.[7] She argues that we are a nuanced and complex combination of nature and nurture. The power of nurture was clearly demonstrated in the #LikeAGirl advertising campaign[8] by Always, the feminine hygiene company, which can be seen on YouTube. Two groups of girls, pre-teens and teenagers, were separately asked to 'run like a girl'. The pre-teens put their heart and soul into it and ran for gold, whilst the teenagers recognised the societal connotations of the phrase 'like a girl' and hammed up their performances, lolling along uselessly. Somewhere between these two stages of growing up, the phrase 'like a girl' had taken on negative connotations, at least in relation to sport.

Boys are subject to a different but equally powerful set of societal messages, arguably pushing them towards behaviour that is physically tough, competitive and individualistic. In *The Hidden Spirituality of Men*[9] Matthew Fox argues that men yearn for

[7] Cordelia Fine, *Delusions of Gender*, Icon Books, 2011.

[8] https://www.youtube.com/watch?v=XjJQBjWYDTs 2014

[9] Matthew Fox, *The Hidden Spirituality of Men: Ten Metaphors to Awaken the Sacred Masculine*, New World Library, 2009.

spiritual experiences but society diverts them with its different expectations, amongst other things rewarding men for their extrovert rather than introvert characteristics, discouraging them from revealing emotions, encouraging the homophobia which prevents them from forming deep friendships with other men; expecting them to focus on work and failing to teach them how to manage rage.

Many of us have found ourselves slipping into gender generalisations whilst simultaneously illustrating that that is precisely what they are: generalisations. Hence comments such as 'He's in touch with his feminine side' or 'She has a very masculine leadership style'. Our awareness that many of the traits usually associated with one particular gender are found in people of the opposite sex, and that socialisation can encourage one sex towards or away from particular behaviours, will caution us against ever making hard and fast judgments about what is a typically male or female behaviour.

The mess in the middle

One central London church has a Ten Point Charter outlining its approach to living the Christian story. The final point tells us, 'We are committed to identifying and affirming what is good and identifying and opposing what is evil, and living as best we can in the mess in the middle'[10]. It is an acknowledgment that life is complex and messy, and certainly not always split into helpfully clear binary categories. Note that the 'mess in the middle' isn't evil, it is just messy.

Today our exploration of what 'male and female', 'masculine and feminine' might mean is enriched by those who experience gender dysphoria: a significant dissonance within themselves regarding the sex assigned to them at birth and sometimes also the roles associated with that sex. Those who transition from one gender to another point up for us the complex social, presentational, biological and hormonal melting pot in which our experiences of gender are forged. If our experience of gender is complex, changing and controversial, involving the struggle to refuse to be constrained by categories, this is mirrored by our experience of being human. At the core of our humanity we know what it is to be uncertain and vulnerable. The philosopher Gillian Rose and more recently Rachel Mann have spoken of 'the broken middle': a way of acknowledging and

---

[10] St Martin-in-the-Fields Church, Trafalgar Square, http://www.stmartin-in-the-fields.org/church/belief/

living with ambiguity, tension, difference and competing truths; the refusal to accept either/or and the recognition that often things are both/and.

The God we are seeking is the God who made a choice to experience the mess and the wonder, the paradox and unknowns, the fragility and questions of human life. If we open our own life journey to the companionship of that God we will be pulled beyond our current understanding and familiar categories towards a wider orientation, away from privilege and boundaries and towards inclusion of experiences and people we don't at first understand.

Widening God's Tent

A theology of inclusion has a very clear biblical basis. In the early days of the Israelites' wanderings in the desert, after the escape from Egypt, they are a community looking for identity. In identity there is coherence and therefore safety and a lack of threat. Deuteronomy 23 sets out strict rules about who is in and who is out of the Lord's assembly, meaning who is welcome in the Lord's tent. Eunuchs, those born of 'an illicit union', and certain tribes are not welcome. In different ways they all threaten Israel's sense of identity, so they are kept at arm's length, part of the wider community but not welcome in the holy space.

By the time we get to the era of the prophets, however, Isaiah chapter 56 is telling us that precisely the eunuchs and foreigners are to be embraced by what is now a community that is confident to embrace otherness rather than perceiving it as a threat. The tent is metaphorically extended.

This extending of God's tent is later lived out in Jesus's radically inclusive relationships with people who were poor and socially marginalised, with those who were sick or dying, with tax collectors and sex workers, with foreigners who worshipped other gods and with women. And the momentum continues as the Gospel reaches beyond Judaism to the Gentiles.

So ours will be an outward-looking theology that is always asking: Who is missing from our community? Who does not feel welcome? Whose voices are not heard and whose gifts and contributions are not accepted? This will by no means just be about women, it will be about social class, educational background, ethnicity, sexuality, political allegiance and many more aspects of our lives which leave some privileged and others excluded.

The author and activist Manal Omar has

said, 'The absence of women is an indicator of larger issues. It is the canary in the coal mine.'[11] We are exploring that particular absence here, because in the history of the Christian faith it is the experiences and voices of women that have often been buried, missing, under-recorded or underplayed. But the point of the exercise is to release in all of us the gifts and characteristics more readily associated with the other gender, that women and men together may discover what it is to be fully human.

What do women bring to the party?

Although there have been notable exceptions it is generally true that the spheres men and women have occupied over the course of history have been different, with men investing much of their energy in the public square and women, probably until the 1920s, giving most of their time and energy to the domestic space. We should pause at this point to state categorically that our domestic lives are not less important than what happens in public, and that what women have done in that space is equally, if differently, significant. We should also say that amongst some of the more questionable

[11] #WhereAreTheWomen event at the Carter Centre, Washington DC, 5 November 2014.

behaviours that may have pertained in public space as shaped by men, there have been innumerable wholly remarkable achievements. Because of this history, when women enter public space they may bring with them a different hinterland,[12] raising issues and making connections that have not been brought to that space before. The psychologist Carol Gilligan suggests that women's voices therefore have a different tone: 'You can't take a life out of history, that life -history and history, psychology and politics, are deeply entwined.' She goes on to say that this 'literally changes the voice: how the human story is told'.[13]

If women's biological and social experience is not explored in our churches we miss out on a whole range of insights into faith and God, including the experience of having been marginalised from public space, and, arguably, a particular tendency, having arrived there, to connect the personal and political. This ability to make connections between different areas of human life can bring a new sense of integration and authenticity. It may also be

[12] An idea explored by Anne Dyer through art and popular culture at the conference of the National Association of Diocesan Advisers in Women's Ministry, 2008.

[13] Carol Gilligan, *In a Different Voice: Psychological Theory and Women's Development*, Harvard University Press, 1982, p.xi.

disruptive, but perhaps creatively so. This is
not a view shared by those who complain about
the 'feminisation of the church'. This is the idea
that men are being put off church by a pastoral
and liturgical style that is too feminine for
their liking because, it is sometimes argued,
it is more relational and less intellectual: as
though those things are mutually exclusive.
William Lane Craig therefore argues that men
need to see Jesus as tough and smart.[14]

The humanisation of the church

Surely the answer is not to emphasise gender
differences in a way that divides, but rather to
embrace a range of human experience together
and to challenge stereotypes rather than
reinforce them as the feminisation argument
does when it promotes a very traditional view
of masculinity such as that described in David
Murrow's *Why Men Hate Going to Church*.[15]
As Jemima Thackray suggests, it may be
that women have not feminised but, rather,
'humanized' the church, and 'If there are those
who feel that the kind of influence which has
broken down domineering power structures

[14] http://www.reasonablefaith.org/the-feminization-of-
christianity, October 2013.

[15] David Murrow, *Why Men Hate Going to Church*, Thomas
Nelson, 2010.

is a threat to the masculinity of that religion, perhaps we should question the version of masculinity they are trying to preserve'.[16]

The Franciscan contemplative and activist Richard Rohr suggests that men and women have different 'entrance points' to spirituality, but that we all end up in the same place because our goal is the same: a deeper relationship with God. 'In the end, a true spirituality is one that affirms men and women at the level of their deepest identity, their true selves in God, an objective and ontological ground – actually much deeper than mere gender, which is always in cultural flux.'[17] He goes on to observe that we all get physically more androgynous as we get older, perhaps pre-figuring a movement beyond gender which will reach its conclusion when we are all taken up into Christ; into the life of God, who both encompasses all gender and is beyond such categories.

If our hope is to 'humanise' our churches in such a way that gender becomes a rich source of thinking and learning about God, then those who are transgender and intersex, people of differing sexualities (see *Sexuality: The*

---

[16] Jemima Thackray, *Telegraph* online, 3 May 2013.

[17] Richard Rohr, 'Gender, God and Spirituality', *Huffington Post*, 28 June 2012.

Inclusive Church Resource[18]) and women and men all have distinctive experiences to offer. So what resources are there from our inheritance in the Christian story which will enable us to redress the balance and engage more fully with the experiences of women?

[18] *Sexuality: The Inclusive Church Resource*, Susannah Cornwall, Darton Longman and Todd, 2014.

CHAPTER 2

Exploring Our Inheritance

An approach to theology

When Christians disagree about the significance and implications of gender the division is not between those who take the Bible seriously and those who sit light to its teachings. In both cases it is the product of rigorous biblical interpretation, one proof of this being that during the past decade or so there has been a revival of interest in gender issues amongst women who might define themselves as 'open evangelical' – or who are influenced by that tradition but would avoid labelling themselves at all.[19]

Some Christians believe that the process of reading scriptural truths across into our own current context is simple and straightforward and requires no cultural interpretation. Our approach however will be to examine the

[19] Rachel Held Evans, *A Year of Biblical Womanhood*, Thomas Nelson, 2012; Sarah Bessey, *Jesus Feminist*, Darton, Longman and Todd, 2013; http://gatheringofwomenleaders. info/

historical context carefully to discern what is timeless and what is culturally constrained. Similarly some Christians take individual verses or passages of scripture separately and interrogate their meaning in isolation from the rest; instead we will try to take account of the overarching themes and the increased understanding which can be traced through the developing Christian tradition.

The texts that we grapple with were written over a period of more than 1500 years, by contributors in numerous communities and cultural contexts. They are a mixture of genres including mythical stories, law, tradition, poetry, gospels (a very particular form of biography), letters to early church communities and accounts of heavenly visions. Given the nature of the texts and our need to apply what we learn to our own context, our understanding will always be emerging and our interpretations provisional.

Theology moving onwards

All Christian theology is a conversation between scripture, the way the Christian story has been told and interpreted over time, and our lived experience and powers of reason. Theology evolves according to the work of God through the Holy Spirit, God's presence in the world. In John's gospel Jesus tells his disciples that after he has gone their understanding of the significance of his life will grow over time: 'I still have many things to say to you, but you cannot bear them now. When the Spirit of truth comes, he will guide you into all the truth.' (John 16:12-13)

The best theology is alive to what God is saying afresh in each generation. There is therefore huge potential for new insights when we see someone from a group of people who were previously excluded fulfilling a particular role, as when a woman presides at Holy Communion. Lucy Winkett refers to the 'religious reductionism' which sees the Eucharist as simply a memorial of something that happened in the past.[20] When a woman presides, simply because she is a woman she signals something other than the repetition and remembering of the Last Supper and a male Jesus. She is reflecting the worship of heaven and of the future.[21]

This idea that our understanding of God develops over time does not cut us loose from any foundational moorings. We are guided in our fresh interpretation of the Gospel by some

[20] Lucy Winkett, 'Why is that priest singing in a woman's voice?', in *Woman*, Nicola Slee and Stephen Burns (eds.), SPCK, 2010, p.99.

[21] Winkett, *Presiding Like a Woman*, p.99.

core understandings that have been tried and tested for two centuries and have held fast, namely: that God creates and sustains the life of the world, that human beings are made in God's image, that the best definition we have of God is 'love', that the thrust of the biblical exploration is towards inclusion, that it is in God's nature to forgive and to reconcile, and that in Jesus we are given a very particular window into what God is like. Bearing all this in mind we turn to some current understandings of gender in the church.

Egalitarians and Complementarians

The two main approaches to a theology of gender in current debate are known as 'egalitarian' and 'complementarian'. Three excellent books explore these approaches in much more detail than we have space for here: *The Gender Agenda* by Lis Goddard and Clare Hendry,[22] *Women and Men in Scripture and the Church* edited by Steven Croft and Paula Gooder[23] and *Equals* by Jenny Baker.[24]

---

[22] Lis Goddard and Clare Hendry, *The Gender Agenda: Discovering God's Plan for Church Leadership*, IVP, 2012.

[23] Steven Croft and Paula Gooder (eds.), *Women and Men in Scripture and the Church: A Guide to the Key issues*, Canterbury Press, 2013.

[24] Jenny Baker, *Equals: Enjoying Gender Equality in All Areas of Life*, SPCK, 2014.

Complementarians believe that women and men are equal in God's sight but have different roles in the church and at home, where men have the final authority. They are relaxed about women holding leadership positions in secular society because they find no biblical material addressing that issue, but many complementarians believe that in church women should exercise leadership only in relation to other women and to children.

Egalitarians believe that God's call to women and men to fulfil any particular role is based not on gender but rather on an individual's gifts, skills and passions. This is the understanding on which this book is based.

One argument used to suggest an intended hierarchy between the sexes is that Eve was created from Adam's rib and is therefore in some sense derived and perhaps does not so closely image God. In fact the Hebrew word for rib can just as appropriately be translated as 'side', implying something more substantial, and to suggest that being derived from Adam makes Eve somehow lesser is inconsistent with Adam being made from dust: he is not hierarchically less than dust!

A second argument suggesting that Eve is in some way subordinate is that in Genesis 2:18 she is described as Adam's 'helper'.

However the word used is *ezer*, which in other places is also used of God, which would rule out any sense of subordination (Genesis 49:25 and Exodus 18:4).

Complementarians argue for different roles for women and men as set out in Genesis 3. However it is only after the Fall that Adam and Eve are assigned different roles involving toil, pain and an unequal relationship. This was not God's original intention and nor is it where the story of how women and men will relate to God and one another ends. Kevin Giles points out that we must look forward to a recreating of the world in Christ (Revelation 21), not backwards to a recapturing of an Eden which was simply the beginning and not the finished product.[25]

Women as agents in the Hebrew Scriptures

In the communities from which the biblical texts emerged it was men who did the writing down. It is possible that in some times and places a woman may have influenced the process, but it was overwhelmingly done by men. It was also men who decided which books were in and which were out of the canon of

---

[25] See Kevin Giles, *The Trinity and Subordinationism: The Doctrine of God and the Contemporary Gender Debate*, IVP, 2002 (Chapter 8 'Exegesis or Eisegesis').

scripture: which became part of the Bible and which were rejected.

The Hebrew Scriptures reflect for the most part a highly patriarchal society, and there are stories which are wholly uncritical of the shocking treatment of women. Phyllis Trible explores some of these in her seminal work *Texts of Terror*, including the abusive treatment of Hagar by Abraham and Sarah (Genesis 16), the rape of Tamar (2 Samuel 13:1-22) and the story of Jephthah's daughter, offered as a burnt-offering as the result of a terrible oath sworn by her father (Judges 11:29-40). Her accounts are uncompromising and her hope is that they will inspire a 'never again' reaction as we shape our own world.[26] The task for us is to ask how the church has at best failed to challenge and at worst fed into the appalling treatment of women and other marginalised groups, and how we might address a whole raft of issues differently today: trafficking, female genital mutilation and domestic abuse, to name just a few.

Alongside these deeply disturbing instances, however, are stories of tenacity, resourcefulness and courage which should be read and explored in our liturgies, preaching

---

[26] Phyllis Trible, *Texts of Terror: Literary Feminist Readings of Biblical Narratives*, Fortress Press, 1984.

and education programmes. We have the wily courage of the midwives Shiphrah and Puah who outwitted Pharaoh's attempt to kill the Hebrew male babies (Exodus 1:15-21); Miriam, who hid her brother Moses in the reeds and ensured his protection by Pharaoh's daughter, led the women in singing and dancing after the crossing of the Red Sea (Exodus 15:20-21) and is considered by Micah to be a leader of Israel (Micah 6:4); and Deborah, the fourth and only female judge of Israel (Judges 4).

Then we have Hannah who sang about the raising up of the marginalised: the song later taken up by the pregnant Mary and known to us as the Magnificat (1 Samuel 2). There is the sheer intensity of maternal love which gave Rizpah the courage to protest against a cruel regime (2 Samuel 21:10-14); the initiative of the young Jewish slave girl of Naaman's wife, who tells him to go to Elisha in order to be healed (2 Kings 5); the bravery of Esther, who rose to the occasion of her 'royal dignity' and risked her life to save her people (Esther 4) and the apocryphal stories of Susannah, who refused to compromise her sexual morality (Daniel 13) and Judith, who challenges the judgment of the elders and articulates for them an alternative theology, a different understanding of God's ways (The Book of Judith).

If we are to take seriously the lives of women today then we need to pay attention to the lives of these women of scripture and others. We might also be inspired by the nameless 'capable wife', found at the end of the book of Proverbs (Proverbs 31:10-31). Held up at times as Superwoman writ large and thereby an unhelpful model, she has been rehabilitated recently by the suggestion that she is a composite figure, illustrative of a whole raft of competencies including those more usually associated with men: business acumen, physical strength, agricultural skill and many others.

Feminine imagery in the Hebrew Scriptures

In the Hebrew scriptures we find metaphorical language about God based in the biology and experience of women. In *She Changes Everything*[27] the author and priest Lucy Reid explores some of these texts, offering us God as mother, midwife and womb. So in Isaiah 42:14 the text describes God's struggles to engage with the beloved nation of Israel like this: 'For a long time I have held my peace, I have kept still and restrained myself; now I will cry out

---

[27] See Lucy Reid, *She Changes Everything: Seeking the Divine on a Feminist Path*, T&T Clark, 2005.

like a woman in labour, I will gasp and pant'. The metaphor is explicitly feminine, related to female biological function, and is unashamed and strong. Again in Isaiah 49:15 'Can a woman forget her nursing-child, or show no compassion for the child of her womb? Even these may forget, yet I will not forget you'. And in Job God is spoken of (by Godself) as having a womb: 'From whose womb did the ice come forth, and who has given birth to the hoar-frost of heaven?'[28]

The significance of inclusive language applied to ourselves and to God is not confined to the question of whether it is helpful to change 'he' to 'she' or 'He' to 'She'. Even if language that assumes male incorporates female does not offend us, nevertheless the experience of suddenly being included can be very powerful. If people don't recognise themselves in the liturgy then their ability to connect with God in themselves and in their daily lives is impoverished. If the stories they hear are always about men and written from a male perspective then both women and men miss out on a wealth of experience and insights. If God is only described in language that is more commonly associated with one gender He may

[28] Job 38:28-29.

continue to feel remote to us, above, beyond and other; rather than here, alongside, and even within.

This applies, too, to the physical images that we see in church: to sculptures and paintings, banners and artwork on service sheets. We have seen that in God both male and female are to be found. If our iconography is unremittingly male then there are areas of our human experience and aspects of our relationship with God that remain unexplored. It can be transforming to explore not just part, but all of what God is and what we might be. It can also have an impact on our approach to other people. The sociologist Andrew Greeley found that belief in a maternal God made Americans less likely to support capital punishment and more likely to favour government help for minority populations and reject the idea that women should remain at home'![29]

In her profoundly thought-provoking book of poetry and prose, the theologian Nicola Slee explores what happens when we envisage the crucified and risen Christ as a woman. She asks why we more readily accept depictions of Christ as having a different ethnic background

---

[29] Cited by Antonia Blumberg in 'The Gender You Associate To God May Indicate How You Feel About Gay Marriage', *Huffington Post*, 16 November 2014.

than Christ as female. She wonders whether the absence of such images connects with the idea that 'women have not realised narratives or images of their own vitality, empowerment and authority'[30]. Perhaps images of a risen female Christ would increase women's ability to see themselves as risen, standing straight and growing into all that they can be.

One of the things that people comment upon when they see a woman lead worship is the theme of 'embodiment'. Men and women are embodied differently, quite literally having bodies that look different. Because that difference is to do with reproductive function, giving birth, feeding a child, it can give rise to a whole different set of thoughts about God. It can also trigger thoughts about ourselves as bodies in relationship with God and not only for women. I recently heard a story about a man who saw his parish priest, who was eight months pregnant, conduct an Advent Service. His reaction was to be overwhelmed by the reality of his own embodiment, saying: 'My faith moved from my head to my whole body'.[31] Turning to the New Testament, what do we

---

[30] Nicola Slee, *Seeking the Risen Christa*, SPCK, 2011, pp. 110-111.

[31] Story told by the Revd Margaret Rose at the Women in Leadership Summit, Liverpool Cathedral, 4 December 2014.

learn about gender from Jesus's relationships with women?

Jesus and Women

There are those who argue that women should not occupy leadership roles in the church because Jesus chose only men to be disciples and was himself a man. In the same way that Virginia Woolf imagined Shakespeare having a sister, Judith, who was as bright and talented as her brother but prevented by her sex from achieving what he did,[32] we can assume that first century Palestinian Judaism would not have engaged with a female Messiah whose disciples were women. Furthermore, in his epic work *The Trinity and Subordinationism*, Kevin Giles argues that 'Surely if the subordination of women is one of the most important distinctives in God's perspective on the man-woman relationship, then Jesus would have raised this matter. The fact that Jesus says not one word on the subordination of women or wives – and that he says and does much that suggests the contrary – convinces me that it is not God's ideal'.[33]

Arguably what is far more remarkable

---

[32] Virginia Woolf, *A Room of One's Own*, 1929.

[33] Kevin Giles, *The Trinity and Subordinationism*, IVP, 2002.

about Jesus than his maleness and choice of male disciples is his inclusion of women in his everyday life and his counter-cultural relationships with some of them. Jesus's life is framed and influenced by women, many of them remarkable. Mary, when we free her from historically questionable assumptions about her meekness and blind obedience, can be seen as what she was: probably a teenager, pregnant and unmarried, she experiences some sort of divine revelation and agrees to bear a child who will belong just as much, if not more, to God as to her. She senses that this birth will be in some sense revolutionary for the world (Luke 1:46-55). Although we hear little about her as Jesus grows up and into his ministry, Mary is key to the changing of water to wine at the wedding at Cana, seemingly pushing Jesus into doing something of which he was doubtful (John 2:3-5), perhaps prompting a new self-understanding; and she is with him to the end, no matter that the end was unspeakable for anyone to witness, especially a parent (John 19:25).

There is another significant point in Jesus's ministry when his self-understanding and perception of his mission changes as a result of a conversation with a woman. Having disputed with the Pharisees about purity laws (Matthew 15:10-11/Mark 7:14-15) Jesus travels to Tyre and Sidon, places which were unfriendly to Jewish people, and there meets a Syro-Phoenician woman, who Matthew refers to as a Canaanite in order to emphasise her 'otherness' and the religious distance between her and Jesus. She asks him to heal her daughter, who has a demon (Mark 7:25-29). Jesus objects that his work is amongst his own people, 'Let the children be fed first, for it is not fair to take the children's food and throw it to the dogs', but she throws the challenge right back: 'Sir, even the dogs under the table eat the children's crumbs.' He heals her daughter and commends her faith. Her intelligence and courage have prompted in him a revelation of the nature of God's indiscriminate love. The Gospel from this point spreads outwards beyond the Jews[34] and Jesus goes on shortly afterwards to feed a crowd of Gentiles (Mark 8).

There is a second remarkable incident with a woman of a different religious commitment in John 4. Joanna Collicutt McGrath notes, 'Jesus makes the first self-revelation of his full divine nature to a Samaritan woman'.[35] He asks the woman for a drink at a well, which would have

---

[34] Joanna Collicutt McGrath, *Jesus and the Gospel Women*, SPCK, 2009, pp. 31-32.

[35] McGrath, *Jesus and the Gospel Women*, p.85.

been a socially and religiously edgy thing to do, and they have a theological conversation about worship. Jesus encourages the woman in her thoughts and reasoning and engages with her as an equal as they effectively banter their way to the revelation that he is the Messiah. There is no sense for this Palestinian Jewish male that women are any less theologically able or spiritually astute than men.

It is clear that a small group of women supported Jesus out of their financial resources and probably travelled with him as they did so (Luke 8:1-3). Some theologians argue that these women were probably present at the Last Supper. Passover meals gathered groups of families and friends, and none of the gospel writers specifically states that only the disciples were present. Certainly some of the women were there at the crucifixion and they turned up the day after the Sabbath to anoint his body. It is apparent that their lives were inextricably bound up with his.

There is also something about embodiment and intimacy which we learn through observing Jesus receiving the touch of women. He comments on the actions of the woman at Bethany – having criticised his male host for a lack of physical welcome – 'You gave me no kiss ... she has not stopped kissing my feet

... her sins, which were many, have been forgiven; hence she has shown great love' (Luke 7:36-50). When he is touched by the woman with a haemorrhage Jesus does not pull away but engages with her (Mark 5:25-34, Luke 8:43-48). We learn an embodied theology through these stories, with Jesus cutting across cultural and religious norms in his willingness towards intimacy.

Various theologians point up Jesus's ability to connect with the worlds that women occupied, both in his conversation with them and also his use of illustrations involving women in his parables and teaching. Thus the widow who gives her mite is held up as exemplary (Mark 12:41-44 and Luke 21:1-4), and God's care of each of his children is depicted as a woman sweeping the house, searching frantically for a lost coin and not resting until it is found (Luke 15:8-10).

Jesus also seems to have the social and emotional insight to know that his words and actions will resonate differently with women and men. Richard Rohr goes so far as to suggest that Jesus shows a markedly different approach in his encounters with the two sexes, and specifically that he is often trying to lift women up and to 'call males downward' if they seem to be a little over-confident in their status.[36] Joanna Collicutt McGrath says something very similar, agreeing that Jesus's actions towards women are often designed literally, figuratively or emotionally to lift them up, whereas there are instances of him challenging men towards greater service and consideration of others.

So Jairus's adolescent daughter is raised, lifted up, from death; the woman bent double is straightened, regaining her dignity and hope, designated a daughter of Abraham (Luke 13:10-17); Mary of Bethany is commended for making the better choice of sitting with Jesus's male listeners, which for her as a woman was something of a promotion, (Luke 10:38-42) and, as beautifully observed by Joanna Collicutt McGrath, Jesus commissions Mary Magdalene to proclaim the Gospel and Peter to a ministry of pastoral care.[37]

Some have asked: because women bring with them some profound experiences of exclusion, not least within the church, how will they make our churches less clerical and our communion more open? Stephen Burns draws out some approaches to leading worship that might arguably grow from this experience,

[36] Richard Rohr, 'Gender, God and Spirituality', *Huffington Post,* 28 June 2012.

[37] McGrath, *Jesus and the Gospel Women,* p.144.

including gestures which are more inclusive, eye contact, preferences for offering communion whilst gathered around the altar rather than queuing[38]. Natalie K Watson speaks of the importance of the Eucharist for those who have been sent away from the table,[39] which connects with the question of whether women and men react differently to phrases used in worship which speak of humility and lack of worth. This will depend, of course, on the individuals, but we might wonder what any undermining of self-worth in church might do, for example, to women already struggling with 'imposter syndrome' in other contexts?

If we do theology from the point of view of a group which has historically been excluded we will encounter these pressure points and triggers that make us think again about our language and concepts, and therefore our understanding of God. Women are again the canary in the coal mine, warning for example that theologies of the cross which emphasise God as a punishing father, exacting revenge, or a merciless judge, will be deeply negative for those who have suffered abuse or inappropriate

---

[38] Stephen Burns 'Four in a Vestment? Feminist gestures for Christian assembly', in *Presiding Like a Woman*, pp. 10-16.

[39] Natalie K. Watson, 'Receiving like a woman', in *Presiding Like a Woman*, p.141.

punishment of any kind. And realising this will fuel our work for gender justice and the righting of wrongs on behalf of all marginalised groups and damaged individuals. We must not separate our understanding of God from the implications it has for all of our brothers and sisters, especially those who are in particular need of being lifted up because they have been dehumanised at the hands of others.

Women and men in the Letters of St Paul

St Paul has often been accused of misogyny. A closer look at his writings suggests something far different. In looking at the relevant texts we need to be aware that in all of his letters to embryonic church communities Paul has one eye on the specific situation which he's addressing and another on how the Gospel might impact on the received cultural norms and habits of the people to whom he is writing.

A number of passages from St Paul's letters allude to the behaviour of women and men in the context of worship. The main bones of contention lie in whether Paul thought it was appropriate at all for women to teach, or even to speak in church; the significance of women being told to dress modestly; whether there is a hierarchy in marriage, with husbands carrying more authority.

Paul's first letter to Timothy, sent to him when he was working with the church in Ephesus addressed a situation where the church was in disarray over issues of doctrine. It is in this context that Paul writes: 'I desire, then, that in every place the men should pray, lifting up holy hands without anger or argument; also that the women should dress themselves modestly and decently in suitable clothing, not with their hair braided, or with gold, pearls, or expensive clothes, but with good works, as is proper for women who profess reverence for God. Let a woman learn in silence with full submission. I permit no woman to teach or to have authority over a man; she is to keep silent' (1 Timothy 2: 8-12).

At first glance this seems absolutely clear: women are subordinate to men in church and must dress modestly. But the word *authentein,* translated as 'have authority over' is rare, and generally conveys an oppressive authority, even coercive or violent. In Ephesus, where the cult of Artemis assured women of equality with men at the very least, Paul may have been warning them against domineering behaviour. Furthermore women did not tend to be educated, and certainly Jewish women

were not permitted to study. This may well
have caused Paul's concern that until they had
learned sound doctrine they were not ready to
teach. Reading this passage through our own
cultural lens we miss the radical nature of
Paul's injunction to let women learn.

It cannot be that Paul intended women
always to remain silent in church, for in the
second passage, 1 Corinthians 11:2-16, he
twice alludes to women prophesying, only
expressing concern at what is worn at the
time: 'any woman who prays or prophesies
with her head unveiled disgraces her head'. In
this same passage he says 'Christ is the head
of every man, and the husband is the head of
his wife, and God is the head of Christ'. This
is notably not a straightforward hierarchical
statement because the order is confused, and
in the same passage Paul tells us both that
'man was not made from woman but woman
from man' and also 'just as woman came from
man, so man comes through woman'. To add
to the complexity of interpretation, theologians
dispute the meaning of the word *kephale*,
translated head: it may connote authority, or
mean 'source' like the head of a river or what
animates and gives life to the body, or mean
'public face'.

With regard to the prescribed dress code

in both the Timothy passage and this one, Paul may well have been simply encouraging women to follow cultural norms rather than draw attention to the emerging church for the wrong reasons. He takes this approach in the preceding passage (1 Corinthians 10) where the appropriate exercise of freedom in the Gospel is about seeking the good of many and being considerate of others, resonating with Jesus's self-emptying for the sake of humanity (Philippians 2:3-11).[40]

In the light of Paul's acceptance that women pray and prophesy in church and his injunction that when they do so they should wear a sign of authority, 1 Corinthians 14:34-35 hits a very jarring note. Here Paul says that women must be silent and subordinate in church for it is shameful for them to speak there. They should ask their husbands at home afterwards if there's something they don't understand. Again there is some contemporary evidence to suggest that the Corinthians at this stage were pretty unruly in worship. It may be that Paul is trying to rein in the habit of people chatting irreverently during worship.

The final passage relating to the behaviour of women and men in Paul's letters is

[40] Lis Goddard and Clare Hendry, *The Gender Agenda*, IVP, 2012.

specifically addressed to wives and husbands and is Ephesians 5:15-33:

'Wives, be subject (*hupotasso*) to your husbands as you are to the Lord. For the husband is the head *(kephale)* of the wife just as Christ is the head *(kephale)* of the church, the body of which he is the Saviour. Just as the church is subject to Christ, so also wives ought to be, in everything, to their husbands. Husbands, love your wives, just as Christ loved the church and gave himself up for her ...' (Ephesians 5:22-25)

Again at first sight this seems to suggest hierarchy, even if the husband is told that his love must be Christ-like. But the word used for head is not *arche*, which would suggest authority, but again *kephale*, which we have seen can mean source, public face or something which animates. *Hupotasso* is also difficult to translate and seems to have more to do with voluntary subjection than anything enforced. Furthermore, verse 21, immediately preceding these injunctions, says quite clearly and mutually: 'Be subject to one another out of reverence for Christ'. If there is mutual subjection then it is hard to see how head can mean 'authority' in the sense of final word.

There were Greek and Jewish household codes in existence at the time which shaped the way that husbands and wives related to one another, together with their children and their servants. Paul seems to have this tradition in mind as he writes to this Greek community and to be framing his picture of appropriate behaviour between wives and husbands within the Greek tradition of male as head and female as body. But if so he redresses the balance a little by stressing the need for men to behave towards their wives with the same care as Christ takes of the church: wives were vulnerable if relationships broke down because they had little status in law.[41] If we interpret the passage as suggesting that the eternal subjection of wives is acceptable then we must also see slavery as acceptable and eternal because Paul does not question it here. But we don't. Rather, we recognise the specific cultural context and the underlying preceding theme of the mutual submission of all believers.

The final controversial passage from St Paul's writings is 1 Timothy 2:8-15, where St Paul seems to suggest that Eve was in some way more responsible for the Fall than Adam was. This idea was taken up by some of the Early Church

[41] Joanne Grenfell, 'Women and Men in Family Life', in *Women and Men in Scripture and the Church: A Guide to the Key Issues*, Stephen Croft and Paula Gooder (eds.), Canterbury Press, 2013.

Fathers and set the scene for the bad press which Eve still receives today. Yet it is difficult to argue this from the biblical texts, where we see that Adam was present when God gave the injunction not to touch the tree of the Knowledge of Good and Evil, but Eve was not: she only had the instruction second-hand, so if anyone was more culpable surely it was Adam. Elsewhere, in fact (Romans 5:14 and 1 Corinthians 15:22), Paul talks about Adam's responsibility for the Fall without even mentioning Eve. Both Genesis and, on balance, Paul would seem to see Adam and Eve as equally responsible and equally bearing the consequences. The church has much to do to rehabilitate Eve and the impact that this has had on the treatment and understanding of women throughout the ages.

We read scripture through our own cultural lens and when it jars with our social norms we can easily miss the nuance, which gets lost in translation. In focussing on the details that we find hard to understand we can also miss the obvious: so although we immediately see that husbands are not asked to be subject to their wives, as Lis Goddard points out no one ever argues that wives do not need to love their husbands because Paul does not ask them to![42]

---

[42] Goddard and Hendry, *The Gender Agenda*.

For those of us left with a niggling sense that it just isn't possible to reconcile these passages it is probably helpful to remember the approach to biblical interpretation which looks for the overarching trajectory of what is revealed in the scriptures, rather than trying to iron out that which can't be ironed. Perhaps the best evidence of Paul's beliefs about women is the way in which he worked with and encouraged them in the early years of the church.

Women as agents in the Early Church

In *Band of Angels* the historian Kate Cooper paints an exciting picture of women occupying visible roles in the early church.[43] As time went on, she observes, they began to focus their energies more on nurturing the good relationships required to sustain these embryonic Christian communities, so that gradually women's names were less likely to be recorded in history whilst men continued to fulfil the more high profile institutional roles. But this shift towards invisibility began we can see from the book of Acts and Paul's letters that women took initiative and played key parts in the emerging church.

---

[43] Kate Cooper, *Band of Angels: The Forgotten World of Early Christian Women*, Atlantic Books, 2013.

So who were these women and what was the nature of their ministry? Some of them were businesswomen who through their trading would have had connections and friendship networks across the Mediterranean world and beyond. One of these women was Lydia, a seller of expensive purple cloth who lived in Philippi. She seems to have welcomed Paul and his friends into her home, resourcing his mission and probably introducing him to contacts in both the Jewish and the Greek communities as she was a Gentile who worshipped God and would therefore have friends in both (Acts 16:13-15).

In Roman colonies such as Corinth women enjoyed legal rights which gave them relative independence compared with those accorded to them under Greek law. Some of them were also effectively in charge of their households and therefore able to influence the propagation of the faith amongst families and networks. Chloe is mentioned as a householder in Corinth whose 'people' have reported quarrels amongst the believers (1 Corinthians 1:10-11). Historians suggest that she probably hosted a church in her house.

In his personal greetings at the end of his letter to the Romans Paul mentions Phoebe, who has apparently carried his letter to Rome: 'I commend to you our sister Phoebe, a deacon of the church at Cenchreae (near Corinth), so that you may welcome her in the Lord as is fitting for the saints, and help her in whatever she may require from you, for she has been a benefactor of many and of myself as well.' By using the words *diakonon*, deacon, and *prostatis*, helper or patron, Paul was emphasising Phoebe's status in the church and encouraging those who received her in Rome to treat her accordingly. It's likely that as well as delivering his letter she helped the Roman Christians to understand it.

Paul had two friends who were his tent-making colleagues, with whom he worked, travelled and possibly lived, Prisca and her husband Aquila. Together the pair correct the teaching of an evangelist called Apollos so that he doesn't convey a distorted version of the Gospel (Acts 18:26). In Romans 16:3-4 Paul mentions that they risked their lives for him and Prisca is, unusually for the cultural mores of the time, mentioned first: Paul seemed to value her friendship and partnership in the Gospel at least as much as Aquila's.

There is then a woman who was imprisoned with Paul, whose name was Junia (Romans 16:7). Some early translators of Paul's letters changed her name to the masculine, Junias, presumably because they could not or did not want to believe that a prominent person named among the apostles was a woman! Euodia and Syntyche are mentioned as leaders of the church in Philippi (Philippians 4:2-3). Paul mentions that they have struggled with him in the work of the gospel, with other co-workers too, and that their names are written in the book of life.

There are other women, particularly those greeted in chapter 16 of Paul's letter to the Romans, of whom we know little more than their names. But when we put these snippets and stories alongside each other we sense the energy of these women and glimpse the formative roles they played in enabling the spread of the Gospel throughout the Mediterranean.

Where did the women go?

Perhaps Kate Cooper is right and the fact that the church's institutional roles were increasingly occupied by men whilst women focussed on the nurture and networking which equally enabled the spread of the Gospel caused women's recorded influence in the church gradually to wane. Women also had the hugely negative legacies of some deeply offensive and unbiblical theology taught by the Early Church Fathers, particularly Augustine, Tertullian and Ambrose. Though we are deeply indebted to these men for some fine theology concerning salvation, the Trinity, the nature of God and more, we also live in the shadow of their deep suspicion of women. This legacy, combined with the dominance of men in the public square means that for much of history until relatively recent times women have been associated 'with the material as opposed to the spiritual, with body rather than mind, with the led rather than the leader' and 'closer to nature, more prone to sin and less rational than men' as well as inferior, needing to be controlled and kept out of sacred space and 'less able to image the divine'.[44]

It is little surprise then that the stories of some biblical women have been indefensibly embellished, and with no historical evidence to support such rumour. So Salome, abused by her mother Herodias as a political tool when she wanted rid of John the Baptist (Mark 6:17-29) has in some strands of art and literature been depicted as an exotic dancer or seductress. In the text she is simply a young girl who does what she is asked by her mother. Mary Magdalene, too, who when she first met Jesus was probably suffering from severe mental health issues, estranged from her family and socially excluded,

[44] Ali Green, 'Being and becoming: How the woman presider enriches our sacred symbols', *Presiding Like a Woman*, Nicola Slee and Stephen Burns (eds.), p. 103.

becomes associated with prostitution.

In spite of all of this there have been women of considerable influence and phenomenal achievement throughout Christian history. Trevor Beeson's book *The Church's Other Half*[45] tells many of their stories. The lives of female saints and martyrs often model what it is to grapple with faith in our daily lives and the politics of our time, and are hugely varied: Marcello the biblical scholar, Paula the linguist who helped Jerome translate the Bible, Hildegard of Bingen with her music, medicine, geology, theology and institutional influence, Julian of Norwich's powerful imagery and intensity of contemplation, Hilda of Whitby with her ability to organise an institution and encourage the gifts of all, including Caedmon whose poetry enriches our tradition. Women are not absent from Christian history, far from it. Their contributions have shaped liturgy, communities and the institution throughout the ages, but often have not been recorded or universally appreciated in their time. In common with our exploration of the Hebrew scriptures there is more work to be done to uncover the riches of their legacy.

[45] Trevor Beeson, *The Church's Other Half: Women's Ministry*, SCM Press, 2011.

CHAPTER 3

How do we raise up women today?

How can we explore this legacy in conversation with our lives here and now? We can begin by immersing ourselves in the stories of women in the Hebrew scriptures, rejoicing in the wisdom, agency and ingenuity of women in patriarchal cultures. We can listen to the Gospel stories with a new awareness of Jesus's counter-cultural relationships with the opposite sex, his intentional 'raising up' of women and their constant presence in his life and ministry. We can re-read Paul's letters with a greater depth of cultural nuance and an awareness of the overall direction in which he is going, and learn from the resourceful women who helped him to spread the Gospel and nurture young church communities.

Then we can pay attention to women and their hinterland, their voices and particular perspectives, at every level in our churches, asking ourselves what they teach us about

God that is new and life-giving, and what it releases and connects with in men. We can allow ourselves to respond with heart, mind and body to the experience of women leading worship. We can explore the theology of the Trinity, of the interweaving dance of God, Creator, Son and Spirit, differentiated yet each fully present in the work of each, in perfect and equal relationship, and ask what it tells us of our human relating.

We can ensure that our churches are led, governed and shaped by women as well as men at all levels. It matters that there is a balance of men to women on working groups and decision-making bodies and contributing to experiences of spiritual formation. When decisions are made, visions are described and dreams are dreamed, women and men need to be in the room. Consideration needs to be given to people's preferred ways of engagement, and to any barriers to participation that women might experience when they sense that they are speaking with a different voice. There also needs to be a vigilant stand against pink Bibles, edited to highlight stories considered suitable for girls, and blue Bibles edited with stories for boys! All of these are ways to end 'the prejudices and practices within the contemporary Church and our society that still keep women in Sarah's place behind the tent-flaps, in a position of having to overhear'.[46]

In conclusion

There are those who would argue that we should by now be beyond conversations about the need to include women and that the church should move on and deal with more pressing issues such as mission, poverty, injustice and the evangelisation of society. That we must, surely, be able to live as though the Kingdom is already here. But whilst the culture in which we worship and relate still has a tendency to consider maleness as normative we are not yet in the Kingdom.

In the words of Pete Wilcox, Dean of Liverpool, speaking at a summit on women in leadership 'Our vision is of a day when every member of our church will be secure in our creation in the image of God, equally male and female; secure in our redemption in Christ's humanity, equally male and female, secure in our mission to the world, in the power of the Spirit, equally male and female. And my prayer for today is that this summit will be a step in the direction of that goal.'[47]

[46] Trevor Dennis, *Sarah Laughed: Women's Voices in the Old Testament*, SPCK, 2010, p.50.

[47] Dean Pete Wilcox, Women in Leadership Summit, Liverpool Cathedral, 4 December 2014.

May our churches have the courage to take intentional steps towards a time when women and men together can fully explore their gendered experience of the world, alongside many other experiences of otherness, and together with the things that all human beings hold in common. And may women never be the gatekeepers but always the extenders of the tent, using their own experience of the mess and miracle of life to engender the humanisation of the church.

Resources

RONNI LAMONT

This resource section compiled by Ronni Lamont will help your church consider how some of the issues raised in the book can be taken further. Here you find a number of small group exercises (which could be used for individual reflection), as well as details of web-based resources.

RONNI LAMONT is a freelance writer and facilitator. Originally a secondary science teacher, she was ordained in 1992, and served in parishes for 16 years. She specialises in (Children's) spirituality, edits www.assemblies. org.uk, and works as a Spiritual Director and supervisor amongst other things. Ronni is the author of Understanding Children, Understanding God, *(SPCK, 2007);* The God Who Leads Us On *(SPCK, 2009) and* Leaping the Vicarage Wall *(Continuum, 2010).*

Small group exercise

'Objectivity is Male Subjectivity.'

Read the article *The rise and fall of Default Man ((pp. 57–72))* , and reflect together about;

1. The description of 'default man'. Is this someone you recognise? Have you ever thought about the (men) who lead western society in this way?

2. Are there female versions of 'default man'? How do you feel about the way they exercise power and authority? How do they differ from/ reflect the 'default men'?

3. Analyse the central committees of your local worshipping community. How powerful is 'default man'? How do you feel about that?

4. Do the 'default men' of your community recognise themselves as such, or do they, as Chris Huhne in the article, see their position as the outcome for individual talent and ability?

5. Now think of the central committees of your part of the Church. How many 'default men' are in power in that place? Are you happy about that, or do you feel powerless to change that ratio? Do you want to?

6. Now imagine how you would like those central and local committees to reflect your community more accurately – who would be there? (You might like to do this activity by drawing, or with post-it notes)

Bible based exercises

Hosea 11

1. When Israel was a child, I loved him,
   and out of Egypt I called my son.
2. The more I* called them,
   the more they went from me;*
   they kept sacrificing to the Baals,
   and offering incense to idols.
3. Yet it was I who taught Ephraim to walk,
   I took them up in my* arms;
   but they did not know that I healed them.
4. I led them with cords of human kindness,
   with bands of love.
   I was to them like those
   who lift infants to their cheeks.*
   I bent down to them and fed them.

Read the passage together and then think about the following;

1. Do you think this is a man or a woman telling their story?
2. Hosea is speaking here as God. Do you think of God as acting in this way with you

– to lift you up and cuddle you as mothers do their children, or fathers do to theirs?

3. Within your concept of God as parent, which parent predominates – is it male or female?

4. Share how you came to have that predominant parent voice of God, and then reflect on how difficult you found it to reflect that way together.

Genesis 1.27:
So God created humankind* in his image,
in the image of God he created them;*
male and *female* he created them.

Genesis 2.23:
Then the man said,
'This at last is bone of my bones
and flesh of my flesh;
this one shall be called *Woman,**
for out of Man* this one was taken

1. In small groups, talk about these two passages, very close to each other in the Bible. Which one do you think reflects equality between the sexes more clearly? What makes you think that?

2. Speaking personally, which one of these two verses indicates more clearly the way that you have experienced life as a male or female?

3. What about the (many) people who would find it hard to categorise themselves as either male

131

or female? Where are they in these passages?

4. Is this non-mention of people who fall outside the traditional gender structure seen within your worshipping community? Or are they welcome and able to be open about who they are?

Proverbs 1.20:

Wisdom cries out in the street;

in the squares she raises her voice.

1. Wisdom is clearly portrayed as feminine in this verse, and indeed throughout the book of Proverbs. Do you usually think of wisdom as a feminine trait? Share together how you feel about wisdom being said to be a feminine trait in this book of the Bible.

2. Wisdom has also been used as a model for the feminine side of the nature of God. Julian of Norwich described Jesus as our Father and Mother. How comfortable are you with seeing the feminine in the Trinity?

Group exercise

1. Issue everyone with three 'post it' notes. Ask them to write one word that they think sums up masculinity on one, and one word for femininity on the other.

2. Take a sheet of flip chart sized paper and draw a line along the bottom. Write the word 'male' on the left hand end, and 'female' on the

right hand end. Now ask everyone to place their two post it notes in that continuum.

3. Now write one word that describes God for you, and place that on the continuum.

4. Sit in a half circle, looking at the continuum, and spend some time contemplating the image of God that the group holds, and pondering if you are comfortable within that place.

General resources:

There are many websites offering advice and help on Gender based issues.

These include;

- Changing Attitude
  www.changingattitude.org.uk
- Gay Christian network
  www.gaychristian.net
- Lesbian & Gay Christian Movement
  www.lgcm.org.uk
- LBGT support online
  www.lgbtnetwork.eu
- *Psychology Today* magazine
  www.psychologytoday.com/basics/gender
- Women and the Church
  www.womenandthechurch.org
- The World Health Organisation
  www.who.int/topics/gender/en

Index

Index